AI Rookies:
Natural Language Processing

Foundations of Text Analytics and NLP

Published by
Data Analytics Curriculum
https://www.dataanalyticscurriculum.com

Supplements and Companion Books

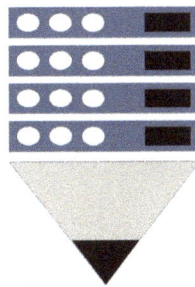

Data Analytics Curriculum

Data Analytics Curriculum, LLC creates approachable, visually engaging educational materials that make data science and AI concepts accessible to learners from high school through college, as well as independent learners.

Our core textbooks—like this one—are sold separately from lab and exercise books so they can be paired with a variety of technologies.

This book is supported by companion lab exercise books for both R (coding-focused) and Orange (no-code), with additional technology options planned for the future.

For more titles, lab books, solution guides, slide decks, and other teaching and learning resources, please visit our store or website:

Website: https://www.dataanalyticscurriculum.com

Contents

Contents

Chapter 1

Introduction to NLP

1-1 Defining NLP

Learning Outcomes

1-1-1 Define Natural Language Processing (NLP) and its role in AI.

1-1-2 Explain why NLP is important for real-world applications.

1-1-3 Describe how linguistics and machine learning support NLP.

Natural Language Processing, or NLP, is a branch of artificial intelligence focused on helping computers understand and work with human language. It involves teaching machines to read, interpret, and even generate language in a way that makes sense to people. By blending computer science, linguistics, and machine learning, NLP allows systems to handle large volumes of text or speech and make sense of it. At its core, NLP is about closing the gap between the way humans communicate and the way machines process information.

Combines
linguistics +
machine learning

Understand &
generate human
language

Powers chatbots,
search,
translation, more

What is NLP?

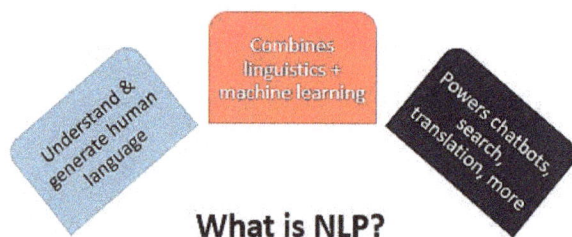

Why NLP Matters in AI

NLP is essential to making AI more human-friendly. It allows software and devices to respond to our questions, understand our commands, and even hold conversations. Whether it's powering a virtual assistant, filtering spam emails, translating languages, or helping businesses analyze customer feedback, NLP is at work behind the scenes. In fields like healthcare and finance, it helps professionals sift through unstructured data quickly and effectively. Simply put, NLP expands what AI can do by giving it the ability to understand and use language—our most powerful tool.

Connection to Linguistics and ML

NLP stands at the intersection of language theory and computational power. From linguistics, it draws on insights about how language works—like grammar rules, meanings of words, and how context affects interpretation. These ideas shape how we design systems that can "read" or "listen" the way people do.

Machine learning brings the ability to learn patterns from massive datasets. Instead of relying only on fixed rules, modern NLP models use algorithms that adapt and improve with more data. Recent advances—especially deep learning and transformer models—have made NLP systems far better at understanding nuance, tone, and context. The collaboration between linguistic understanding and machine learning techniques is what drives progress in this field.

Review Questions

1. What is NLP and what does it aim to do?
2. Why is NLP important in AI applications?
3. Name two industries where NLP is used.
4. How do linguistics and machine learning contribute to NLP?

1-2 Common Tasks in NLP

Learning Outcomes

1-2-1 Identify key tasks in NLP such as tokenization, parsing, and sentiment analysis.

1-2-2 Explain what each task does and why it's important.

1-2-3 Recognize real-world applications of common NLP tasks.

NLP encompasses a wide range of tasks that allow machines to process and understand language.

Tokenization

Tokenization is the process of breaking text into smaller units, such as words or sentences. This is a fundamental step in NLP, as it helps structure raw text data into manageable pieces for further processing.

For example, the sentence "Natural Language Processing is fun!" can be tokenized into words: "Natural", "Language", "Processing", "is", "fun". This helps a computer process each word individually.

Parsing

Parsing involves analyzing the grammatical structure of a sentence to figure out relationships between words. This can include syntactic parsing (finding sentence structure) and dependency parsing (figuring out relationships between words).

For example, in the sentence "The cat sat on the mat," syntactic parsing identifies the sentence structure: "The cat" is the noun phrase (subject), "sat on the mat" is the verb phrase. Dependency parsing shows how words relate: "sat" is the main verb, "cat" is the subject linked to "sat," and "on the mat" is a prepositional phrase modifying "sat."

Named Entity Recognition (NER)

NER is the task of finding and classifying entities in text, such as names of people, organizations, locations, dates, and other predefined categories. This is widely used in applications such as information extraction and search engines.

Sentiment Analysis

Sentiment analysis figures out the emotional tone of a text, classifying it as positive, negative, or neutral. This is commonly used in social media monitoring, customer feedback analysis, and brand reputation management.

For example, the sentence "I love this product!" would be classified as positive, while "This is the worst experience ever." would be labeled negative. Sentiment analysis helps companies quickly understand how people feel about their brand.

Machine Translation

Machine translation involves automatically translating text from one language to another. Advanced NLP models, such as Google's Neural Machine Translation (GNMT), have significantly improved translation accuracy.

Speech Recognition

Speech recognition converts spoken language into text, enabling applications such as virtual assistants (e.g., Siri, Alexa) and automated transcription services.

Text Summarization

Text summarization generates concise summaries of longer documents while preserving key information. This is useful for news aggregation, research papers, and legal document analysis.

Chatbots and Conversational AI

NLP powers chatbots and conversational agents that can engage in human-like conversations. These systems are widely used in customer support, personal assistants, and e-commerce.

Review Questions

1. What is tokenization, and why is it important in NLP?
2. How does parsing help a machine understand sentence structure?
3. What kinds of information does Named Entity Recognition extract?
4. What is sentiment analysis used for?
5. How does machine translation apply NLP in real life?
6. Name two uses of speech recognition.
7. Why is text summarization useful?

1-3 History and Evolution of NLP

Learning Outcomes

1-3-1 Describe how NLP has changed over time.

1-3-2 Explain what rule-based, statistical, machine learning, and transformer methods are.

1-3-3 Recognize important models like BERT and GPT and what they do.

1-3-4 Understand how these changes made NLP better and more useful.

Rule-Based Approaches

In the early days of Natural Language Processing (NLP), most systems relied on manually crafted rules to interpret language. These rule-based or symbolic approaches were built around predefined grammar rules and vocabulary lists. Developers would write specific instructions for how the computer should process words, phrases, and sentence structures.

One well-known example was the Georgetown-IBM experiment in 1954, which used a set of rules to translate Russian into English. While this showed that machines could work with language, it quickly became clear that this method had limits. Human language is full of nuance, context, and ambiguity that rigid rules can't easily capture. These early systems worked reasonably well on narrowly defined tasks but struggled when faced with more varied or unpredictable language.

NLP Over Time

Rules – Hand-coded logic

Machine Learning – Learn from data

Transformers – BERT, GPT

Statistics – Word patterns

Deep Learning – Neural networks

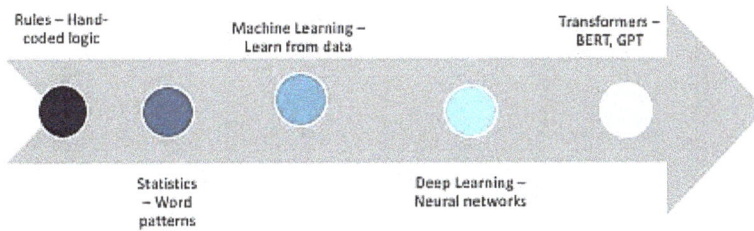

From Rules to Statistics

By the 1980s and 1990s, the field began shifting away from hand-coded rules toward data-driven approaches. As computers became more powerful and access to text data increased, researchers began applying statistical techniques to language. This meant using large datasets to estimate probabilities and patterns, rather than writing rules by hand.

Hidden Markov Models (HMMs) and n-gram models have become common tools for tasks like tagging parts of speech, recognizing speech, and translating languages. A major milestone was the development of IBM's statistical machine translation models in the early 1990s, which relied on bilingual corpora to learn how words from one language correspond to another.

Statistical methods made NLP more flexible and scalable. Instead of trying to anticipate every possible sentence structure, these models could learn from examples and adapt to new language patterns.

Rise of Machine Learning and Deep Learning

In the 2000s, machine learning started playing a bigger role in NLP. Algorithms like Support Vector Machines (SVMs), Conditional Random Fields (CRFs), and Latent Dirichlet Allocation (LDA) allowed systems to learn directly from data—reducing the need for manual intervention. These methods improved how computers could classify text, analyze sentiment, and discover topics in documents.

The biggest leap came in the 2010s with the arrival of deep learning. Using neural networks, researchers developed models that could process sequences of text and capture complex relationships between words. Recurrent Neural Networks (RNNs), Long Short-Term Memory (LSTM) networks, and Convolutional Neural Networks (CNNs) led to major advances in how machines understand language.

This era also brought Neural Machine Translation (NMT), which outperformed older statistical models by using entire sentences as input rather than translating word by word. The shift to deep learning dramatically improved accuracy in translation, question answering, and many other NLP tasks.

Recent Breakthroughs with Transformer Models

In recent years, transformer models have dramatically changed the landscape of Natural Language Processing. Originally introduced in the landmark 2017 paper *"Attention Is All You Need"* by Vaswani and colleagues, the transformer architecture moved away from the step-by-step processing used by earlier neural networks. By allowing for parallel computation, transformers made it faster and more efficient to analyze and understand language.

One of the first major successes built on this architecture was BERT (Bidirectional Encoder Representations from Transformers), released by Google in 2018. BERT stood out because it reads text in both directions—left to right and right to left—giving it a better sense of context around each word. This approach significantly improved results in tasks like answering questions and identifying named entities.

OpenAI's GPT series (Generative Pre-trained Transformer) took a different approach. Rather than analyzing language in both directions like BERT, GPT uses a unidirectional (left-to-right) model and focuses on generating text. With each new version—GPT-2, GPT-3, and GPT-4—the quality of the generated language has grown more fluent and coherent, making these models powerful tools for writing, summarizing, and conversation.

Other models, like T5 (Text-to-Text Transfer Transformer) and XLNet, have built on this momentum by introducing new training strategies and architectural improvements. These systems have pushed the performance of NLP tools across many different tasks, from translation to document classification.

Transformers have become the foundation of modern NLP. Their ability to understand language in rich, contextual ways continues to open doors for more intuitive, human-like interactions between people and machines.

Review Questions

1. What were rule-based NLP systems, and why didn't they work well for complex language?
2. How did statistical models help NLP improve?
3. What is one example of a statistical model used in the 1990s?
4. How did machine learning change NLP in the 2000s?
5. What are neural networks, and how did they help with understanding language?
6. What is a transformer model?
7. How does BERT understand word meaning better than earlier models?
8. What can GPT models do?
9. How have newer NLP models changed how computers interact with people?

1-4 Key Challenges in NLP

Learning Outcomes

1-4-1 Identify common challenges in understanding natural language.
1-4-2 Explain why context, ambiguity, and different languages make NLP difficult.
1-4-3 Describe issues related to bias and fairness in NLP models.
1-4-4 Understand how computational limits affect large NLP systems.

Ambiguity Makes NLP Hard

One of the toughest hurdles in Natural Language Processing (NLP) is dealing with ambiguity—the fact that words and sentences often have more than one possible meaning. This can happen in several ways. A single word might have multiple meanings (lexical ambiguity), a sentence might be interpreted in different ways depending on how it's structured (syntactic ambiguity), or the overall meaning might just be unclear without more context (semantic ambiguity).

Take this sentence: *"I saw the man with the telescope."* Does it mean the speaker used a telescope to see the man, or that the man had a telescope? People can usually figure it out based on real-world experience or context. Computers, however, don't come with that kind of background knowledge, which makes resolving ambiguity especially tricky.

Context and Meaning Matter

To understand language the way people, do, NLP systems need to grasp not just the words, but the context around them. Meaning often depends on what came before in a conversation—or even what's implied but not said directly. Idioms, jokes, sarcasm, and figurative language all rely on subtle cues that can be hard for machines to interpret.

For example, when someone says *"kick the bucket,"* we know it means "to die," not literally kicking a bucket. But a machine that only understands literal meanings could get confused. Even with advances like transformers and large language models, fully understanding context—especially over longer conversations—is still a work in progress. These systems need a lot of data and training to handle the wide range of expressions found in real language.

Challenge of Languages and Dialects

Languages around the world don't all work the same way. Some use complex word forms to express meaning, like Turkish or Finnish, where a single word might carry the information that English would spread across several words. In addition, dialects within a single language can vary dramatically, using different vocabulary, grammar, or expressions.

While modern NLP tools have made great progress in English and other high-resource languages, many systems struggle when applied to languages with fewer resources or less labeled data. Creating language models that can work reliably across different languages and dialects remains a major goal—and a major challenge—in the field of NLP.

Why NLP is Hard

- Ambiguity
- Context matters
- Bias in data
- Language variety
- High compute cost

Ethical Challenges and Bias in NLP Systems

As NLP technologies become more widely used, the issue of bias in language models has become increasingly important. These systems learn from huge amounts of online text, which often reflects the biases and stereotypes found in society. For instance, a model trained on unfiltered data might associate certain careers more often with one gender or reflect cultural and racial prejudices found in public discourse.

Such biases don't just stay in the data—they show up in the outputs, which can result in offensive or unfair responses from AI systems. This is especially concerning when NLP tools are used in sensitive areas like hiring, law enforcement, or healthcare. While researchers are working on ways to detect and reduce bias—through better data curation and algorithmic fairness—it's a complex problem, and creating completely neutral models is still out of reach.

Limits of Computational Power in NLP

Cutting-edge NLP models like GPT and BERT are incredibly powerful—but they come at a cost. Training and running these systems require a massive amount of computing power, specialized hardware, and huge datasets. This makes it expensive to build and maintain, and it puts them out of reach for many smaller organizations or developers.

There's also the issue of scaling. Many NLP models are designed to run on high-end servers, but not every application has that luxury. Adapting these systems to work on smartphones, low-power devices, or in real-time can be difficult. Researchers are exploring solutions like model compression, knowledge distillation, and more efficient architectures to make NLP more accessible. Still, finding the right balance between performance and resource use remains a major challenge.

Review Questions

1. What does it mean when language is ambiguous? Give an example.
2. Why is understanding context important in NLP?
3. What are some difficulties when building NLP systems for different languages and dialects?
4. How can NLP models show bias, and why is that a problem?
5. What are the challenges of using large models like GPT or BERT in real-world applications?

1-5 Real-World Applications of NLP

Learning Outcomes

1-5-1 Identify key NLP applications like translation and sentiment analysis.

1-5-2 Explain how NLP powers tools like chatbots and virtual assistants.

1-5-3 Describe how NLP supports search engines and speech recognition.

1-5-4 Recognize NLP's role in business, healthcare, and daily life.

1-5-5 Understand the impact of NLP on communication and automation.

Machine Translation

Machine translation is one of the most recognized and practical applications of Natural Language Processing (NLP). It enables text or speech to be automatically translated from one language to another, breaking down communication barriers around the world. Tools like Google Translate, Microsoft Translator, and DeepL have made it possible for people to access information and connect across languages with ease.

Earlier translation systems depended on rule-based logic or statistical models, which often produced stiff or inaccurate translations. Today, the landscape has shifted thanks to neural machine translation (NMT), a deep learning approach that produces smoother, more natural output by understanding full sentence structures rather than translating word by word.

For example, Google Translate uses the Transformer architecture breakthrough in deep learning that significantly enhances translation quality by modeling context across entire sentences. Modern systems can also handle multiple languages at once, even without direct pairwise training data, thanks to multilingual models. As a result, machine translation now plays a central role in business communication, international travel, academic research, and diplomacy, making global interaction more seamless than ever before.

Sentiment Analysis

Sentiment analysis, sometimes called opinion mining, is another key area in NLP that focuses on detecting the emotional tone of written text. It's widely used across industries to understand how people feel about a product, brand, or event. Companies rely on sentiment analysis to monitor customer satisfaction, analyze product reviews, and track the public's reaction to marketing campaigns.

Using advanced NLP techniques, sentiment analysis tools can classify text as positive, negative, or neutral—and in more advanced cases, even detect subtleties like sarcasm or conflicting emotions. For example, businesses monitor platforms like Twitter, Instagram, and Facebook to track public opinion in real time and quickly respond to concerns or praise. Politicians, too, use sentiment data to measure voter sentiment and adjust their messaging.

In finance, sentiment analysis helps analysts gauge market mood by evaluating investor commentary and news headlines. As AI continues to improve, sentiment analysis is becoming more sophisticated, helping organizations uncover deeper emotional insights from vast amounts of unstructured text.

Chatbots and Virtual Assistants

Chatbots and virtual assistants are among the most familiar and widely used applications of Natural Language Processing (NLP). These tools interact with users through natural language, answering questions, helping, and completing tasks—often in real time. Many businesses use chatbots for customer service, allowing them to respond to frequently asked questions, handle support requests, and reduce the workload on human agents.

Virtual assistants like Apple's Siri, Amazon's Alexa, and Google Assistant go even further. They interpret voice commands and can perform a wide range of actions, from sending messages to controlling smart home devices. What makes these systems effective is their ability to understand intent, remember the context of conversations, and respond in a way that feels natural.

Recent improvements in deep learning—especially transformer-based models—have made these interactions more fluid and human-like. You'll now find chatbots being used in healthcare to answer patient questions, in banking to help with account inquiries, and in e-commerce to guide customers through product searches and purchases. As virtual assistants continue to evolve, they're becoming a central part of smart living environments, helping users manage everything from to-do lists to thermostat settings with just their voice.

Speech Recognition

Speech recognition technology allows machines to turn spoken language into written text, enabling more natural ways for people to interact with computers. This is the core of voice-to-text systems used in transcription services, mobile apps, and digital assistants. It also plays a vital role in improving accessibility for people with disabilities.

Apps like Google Voice Typing, Apple's Siri, and Microsoft's Cortana make it easy to dictate messages, search the internet, and issue commands without using a keyboard. Behind the scenes, these systems rely on sophisticated NLP techniques and deep learning models—especially recurrent neural networks (RNNs) and transformers—to interpret speech accurately and in context.

Speech recognition is especially valuable in industries like customer service, where interactive voice response (IVR) systems help automate and route calls efficiently. It's also widely used in the legal and medical fields, where professionals rely on accurate voice-to-text tools to create transcripts, document notes, and streamline their workflows. As technology continues to improve, speech recognition is becoming faster, more accurate, and more deeply integrated into daily life.

Information Retrieval

Information retrieval is another critical application of NLP, empowering search engines like Google, Bing, and Yahoo to deliver relevant results based on user queries. Search engines use sophisticated NLP algorithms to understand user intent, analyze keywords, and rank web pages based on relevance.

Modern search engines incorporate semantic search capabilities, enabling them to go beyond simple keyword matching and understand the contextual meaning behind queries. Technologies such as Google's BERT (Bidirectional Encoder Representations from Transformers) have significantly improved search accuracy by enhancing language comprehension.

Information retrieval is not limited to web search engines; it also plays a vital role in enterprise knowledge management systems, academic databases, and e-commerce platforms. Companies use NLP-powered search functions to retrieve product information, legal documents, and research articles efficiently. As NLP continues to evolve, search engines will become even more intuitive, providing users with highly exact and contextually relevant information.

Healthcare Applications

Natural Language Processing (NLP) has transformed healthcare by enabling swift and accurate analysis of medical text data. Whether it's electronic health records (EHRs), clinical notes, or research articles, NLP-powered tools help improve patient outcomes, support clinical decisions, and reduce administrative workload.

A key application lies in medical text analysis, where NLP extracts critical details from unstructured sources such as doctors' notes, pathology reports, and scientific literature. These systems can identify diseases, symptoms, and treatment options, providing valuable insights that assist healthcare professionals in diagnosis and care planning.

NLP also plays an important role in drug development and safety monitoring. By mining extensive datasets—including clinical trial results, published studies, and patient reports—NLP helps researchers spot potential drug interactions, adverse reactions, and emerging health patterns more efficiently.

Patient engagement is another growing area where NLP-powered chatbots and virtual health assistants offer significant benefits. These AI-driven tools provide medical advice, help schedule appointments, and offer symptom assessments, easing the load on healthcare providers and making healthcare more accessible to patients.

Review Questions

1. How does Google Translate use NLP to improve translations?
2. What is sentiment analysis, and why do businesses use it?
3. Give an example of how chatbots or virtual assistants use NLP.
4. How does speech recognition help people in daily life or work?
5. How is NLP used in healthcare to help doctors and patients?

Chapter 2

Text Preprocessing

2-1 Raw Text Data

Characteristics

Raw text is both rich and unruly. Unlike structured data—which fits neatly into tables and columns—text arrives without any fixed format. It doesn't follow clear patterns or categories, and there's no built-in labeling system. Instead, it unfolds in sentences and paragraphs, shaped by the writer's intent and language style. This lack of structure makes it difficult for computers to make sense of the content unless it's first cleaned and transformed using natural language processing tools.

One of the biggest challenges with raw text is the sheer number of ways ideas can be expressed. A single concept might appear in dozens of wordings, with different spellings, synonyms, or grammatical forms. Words like "large" and "big" mean roughly the same thing but may not be treated that way by simple algorithms. This makes text data highly complex and "high-dimensional"—meaning there are countless possible words and combinations to account for. To tame this complexity, researchers often turn to tools like word embedding or dimensionality reduction, which help organize language into more manageable forms.

Characteristics of Raw Text

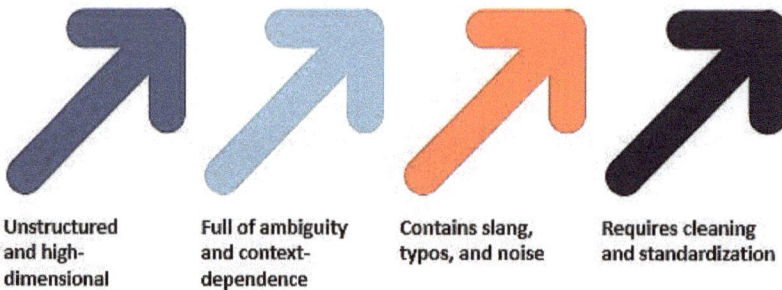

| Unstructured and high-dimensional | Full of ambiguity and context-dependence | Contains slang, typos, and noise | Requires cleaning and standardization |

Another issue is noise. Raw text tends to be messy, especially in informal settings like social media. You'll often encounter misspellings, slang, emojis, abbreviations, and inconsistent grammar. Even in more polished writing—like news stories or legal texts—there can be irregular formatting or shifts in terminology. Before analysis, this messiness needs to be cleaned up through techniques such as spell correction, lemmatization, and stemming.

Context also plays a big role in how words function. The same word can mean very different things depending on where and how it's used. "Apple," for instance, might refer to fruit or a tech company depending on the sentence. Even verbs like "run" take on different meanings in phrases like "run a business" versus "run a mile." Because of these shifting meanings, advanced

NLP systems like BERT are designed to interpret words based on the words around them rather than treating each term in isolation.

Finally, text can vary in language and style. People write in many different languages, and sometimes they mix languages in the same sentence. The tone may shift from formal to casual, or from personal to technical, all within the same dataset. These stylistic and linguistic shifts add another layer of complexity for machines trying to make sense of raw language.

Challenges in Text Processing

Working with raw text comes with a set of difficulties, largely because it doesn't follow any fixed format. Unlike structured data—where everything fits neatly into rows and columns—text data is free-form, full of ambiguity, and shaped by how people naturally communicate. Analyzing this kind of data requires extra effort up front to prepare it, and even then, the subtleties of language can make things tricky. If those subtleties aren't accounted for, the results of the analysis can be misleading or incorrect.

One persistent issue is that many words have more than one meaning. Take the word "bank"—it might mean a place to keep money or the edge of a river, depending on how it's used. Figuring out the correct meaning in each case isn't easy and calls for models that understand context, not just individual words. That's where more advanced language tools—like deep learning models trained on huge collections of text—come into play. Without that level of context-awareness, software may get confused, especially in tasks like answering questions, detecting sentiment, or retrieving information.

Another challenge comes from the fact that people often say the same thing in different ways. For instance, "glad" and "joyful" carry similar meanings, but unless a model knows how those words relate, it might treat them as unrelated. This is a problem for any task that relies on understanding meaning—like grouping documents, retrieving search results, or translating text. To handle this, systems often use word representations (like Word2Vec or BERT) that learn word relationships based on how they're used in real writing.

The messiness of real-world text is another complication. People misspell words, use abbreviations, write in slang, and break grammar rules—especially online. A tweet, for example, might contain emojis, hashtags, and half-formed sentences. All of this "noise" makes it harder for machines to analyze the text accurately. To fix this, the data must be cleaned first—by correcting spelling, reducing words to their roots, and standardizing different forms of the same word.

The lack of built-in structure adds another layer of difficulty. Structured data already comes labeled and sorted—text doesn't. To make sense of it, we must apply techniques like identifying people's names or places, tagging parts of speech, and breaking sentences down into their grammatical components. These steps help uncover the hidden structure within the text and make it more useful for building tools like recommendation engines or digital assistants.

Another issue arises when text contains more than one language. It's common, especially in bilingual communities, to see a sentence that mixes languages—something known as code-switching. For example, "Voy al mall para comprar ropa" blends Spanish and English. This makes analysis harder for models trained in just one language. Handling such text requires specially trained multilingual tools, which makes the process more complex.

Finally, there's the scale of the problem. Text data tends to be huge—think about the size of online reviews, emails, social media feeds, and entire libraries of documents. Analyzing all that takes serious computing power. Techniques like parallel processing, cloud computing, and smart algorithms help manage the load, but they also raise costs and add technical challenges. That's why methods like topic modeling and dimensionality reduction are so valuable—they help reduce the size of the problem while keeping the important details intact.

Common Sources of Text Data

Sources of Text Data

Social media	• casual, noisy
News	• formal, edited
Reviews	• opinion-heavy
Emails, chat logs	• sensitive, informal
Scientific/legal texts	• technical, structured

Text data is everywhere, generated continuously across a wide variety of platforms and contexts. One of the most active sources is social media. Sites like Twitter, Reddit, and Facebook produce massive volumes of user content—tweets, comments, posts, and conversations—every day. This kind of data reflects a wide range of topics and tones, from everyday opinions to breaking news. Because social media often uses casual, unfiltered language—complete with slang, emojis, abbreviations, and hashtags—it can be tricky to analyze. Still, it's a valuable resource for monitoring public opinion, tracking events as they unfold, and identifying misinformation.

News outlets are another major source of raw text. Online news sites publish articles covering politics, science, entertainment, and global affairs. Unlike social media, this content tends to be polished and formal, with clearer grammar and structure. As a result, news texts are useful for tasks like summarizing long passages, recognizing named entities (like people and places), and organizing content by topic. Although news articles typically go through editorial review, the rapid spread of online news has raised concerns about accuracy and bias—leading to increased interest in automatic fact-checking systems.

Customer reviews are also an important source of text, especially for companies that want to understand how people feel about their products and services. Platforms like Amazon, Yelp, and TripAdvisor host countless reviews written by users. These reviews can reveal customer satisfaction, feature requests, or common complaints. Businesses often apply sentiment analysis to this kind of data to improve their offerings. Still, like social media, reviews can be messy, with spelling mistakes, emotional language, and even fake entries that must be filtered out.

Text also flows through communication tools—like email, instant messaging, and team collaboration apps. Services such as Slack, Microsoft Teams, and email clients hold vast stores of written exchanges. This type of data is useful for improving customer service, detecting spam, or analyzing patterns of communication in the workplace. However, privacy concerns mean this data must be handled with care, particularly when it contains sensitive or confidential information.

Scientific and medical writing makes up another important category of text. Research articles, clinical notes, technical reports, and medical case files contain dense, specialized language. These texts are essential for research in healthcare, pharmacology, and other fields. Analyzing them can support clinical decisions or identify trends across studies. But because the vocabulary is highly technical and domain-specific, specialized tools and careful preprocessing are required to make the information usable.

Finally, legal and financial texts—like contracts, court rulings, annual reports, and compliance documents—form a large and valuable body of language data. These documents often follow formal writing conventions and include precise, structured wording. Text analysis in these fields can help with tasks like reviewing contracts, identifying risk factors, or spotting patterns in regulatory filings. That said, the complexity and formatting of these documents require advanced tools capable of parsing dense, rule-based language.

Importance of Preprocessing

Why Preprocessing is Essential

Removes noise and redundancy

Prepares text for modeling

Boosts NLP accuracy and efficiency

Before any meaningful analysis can begin, raw text must be cleaned up and prepared. This step—known as preprocessing—is essential in any NLP pipeline. Real-world text often includes typos, inconsistent formatting, re-peated phrases, and irrelevant material. If left unaddressed, these issues can confuse models and reduce the quality of the results.

Preprocessing helps resolve these problems by standardizing the text and removing noise. Techniques such as tokenization, lowercasing, removing punctuation, correcting spelling, and reducing words to their base form (like stemming or lemmatization) turn messy input into something structured and consistent. With well-prepared data, NLP models are more accurate, effi-cient, and easier to train. Without it, even the most sophisticated algorithms may produce unreliable results.

Review Questions

1. What makes raw text data unstructured?
2. Why is high dimensionality a challenge in text data?
3. Give two examples of noise in text.
4. What does it mean that text is context-dependent?
5. How do synonyms affect analysis?
6. What is code-switching?
7. Why is preprocessing important?

2-2 Tokenization

Learning Outcomes

2-2-1 Define tokenization and explain its role in NLP.

2-2-2 Distinguish between word, sentence, and subword tokenization.

2-2-3 Recognize challenges in tokenizing different languages and text types.

2-2-4 Describe BPE and WordPiece subword methods.

2-2-5 Compare tokenization tools: NLTK, spaCy, Hugging Face.

2-2-6 Choose appropriate tokenization strategies for NLP tasks.

Definition and Importance

Tokenization is a fundamental process in Natural Language Processing (NLP) that involves breaking text into smaller, meaningful units called tokens. These tokens can be words, sentences, subwords, or even characters, depending on the level of granularity needed for a given NLP task. Tokenization serves as a critical preprocessing step in text analysis, enabling machines to interpret and process human language more effectively.

The importance of tokenization lies in its ability to structure unprocessed text, making it suitable for further computational analysis. Without tokenization, text remains a continuous sequence of characters that lacks clarity in terms of individual words or sentences. Tokenization helps various NLP applications, including text classification, sentiment analysis, machine translation, and information retrieval. By segmenting text appropriately, tokenization ensures that later NLP models can efficiently extract meaning, find patterns, and generate correct predictions.

Types of Tokenization

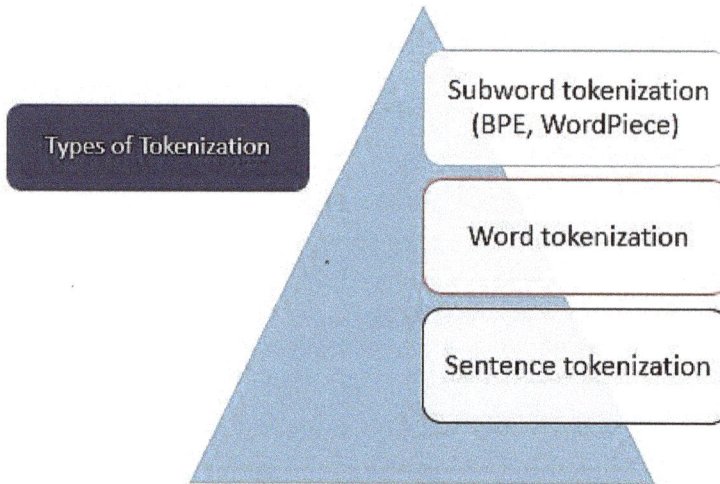

Tokenization is a fundamental step in natural language processing (NLP) that involves breaking text into smaller units for analysis. Depending on the level of segmentation, tokenization can be categorized into three main types: word tokenization, sentence tokenization, and subword tokenization. Each type serves a specific purpose and comes with its own set of challenges.

Word Tokenization

Word tokenization, also known as lexical tokenization, involves splitting text into individual words. This is one of the most used tokenization techniques, where a sequence of text is segmented based on spaces, punctuation marks, or language-specific rules.

For example, given the sentence:

"I saw the sign."

A simple word tokenization process would generate the following tokens:

"I", "saw", "the", "sign"

While word tokenization is straightforward in languages that use spaces between words, it faces challenges with contractions (e.g., "can't" being split into "can" and "not"), hyphenated words, and languages like Chinese and Japanese that do not separate words with spaces. Special handling techniques, such as dictionary-based segmentation, are needed for these cases.

Sentence Tokenization

Sentence tokenization, also known as sentence segmentation, involves dividing text into individual sentences. This technique is particularly useful in applications such as text summarization, machine translation, and sentiment analysis, where understanding sentence boundaries is essential.

For example, given the text:

"Tokenization is an important first step in NLP. It helps in text analysis and machine learning."

A sentence tokenizer would produce:

"Tokenization is an important first step in NLP." "It helps intext analysis and machine learning."

Despite its usefulness, sentence tokenization can be challenging due to the presence of abbreviations (e.g., "Dr.", "U.S.") and varying punctuation rules across different languages. Advanced models use rule-based approaches and machine learning techniques to accurately detect sentence boundaries.

Subword Tokenization

Subword tokenization is an advanced technique that splits words into smaller, meaningful subunits. This approach is particularly beneficial for handling out-of-vocabulary (OOV) words, reducing vocabulary size, and improving model efficiency. Two widely used subword tokenization methods are Byte Pair Encoding (BPE) and WordPiece.

Byte Pair Encoding (BPE) is a data-driven subword segmentation technique that iteratively merges the most often occurring character pairs into subwords. This method is widely used in machine translation and large-scale NLP models.

For instance, the word *"unhappy"* might be tokenized as:

"un", "happy"

This approach allows models to recognize common word structures and generalize across different words, improving their ability to process rare and complex terms.

WordPiece, another subword tokenization method, is commonly used in transformer-based models like BERT. It segments words into subword units based on frequency statistics, refining vocabulary efficiency.

For example, the word *"playing"* might be tokenized as:

"play", "ing"

By breaking words into frequent subunits, WordPiece enables language models to better handle rare words and morphological variations.

Tokenization Tools and Libraries

Available tools and libraries (available in R and Python and other languages and applications) provide robust implementations of tokenization techniques, making it easier for developers and researchers to process text efficiently. These libraries offer pre-built functions and models designed to manage various tokenization challenges across different languages and applications.

One of the most widely used tokenization libraries is NLTK (Natural Language Toolkit). As one of the earliest and most comprehensive NLP libraries for Python, NLTK provides efficient methods for both word and sentence tokenization. It uses rule-based heuristics to split text into meaningful units, making it a popular choice for academic research and basic text processing tasks. Due to its simplicity, NLTK is often used in introductory NLP applications and educational settings.

Another powerful tokenization library is spaCy, which is known for its speed and efficiency. Unlike NLTK, spaCy uses pre-trained tokenization models that are specifically tailored for multiple languages. This makes it is highly effective for handling complex linguistic structures, including contractions and multi-word expressions. SpaCy has useful applications due to its optimized performance and ability to integrate with other NLP pipelines, such as named entity recognition and dependency parsing.

For deep learning applications, Hugging Face Tokenizers is one of the most advanced tokenization libraries available. It is designed specifically for modern NLP models and supports tokenization strategies such as WordPiece and Byte Pair Encoding (BPE). This library is commonly used for processing text in transformer-based models like BERT, GPT, and T5. By using efficient tokenization techniques, Hugging Face enables better handling of rare words, subword segmentation, and multilingual text processing.

Each of these tokenization tools serves a unique purpose, and the choice of library depends on the specific requirements of a given NLP task. While NLTK is suitable for traditional text processing, spaCy provides optimized performance for large-scale applications, and Hugging Face Tokenizers are essential for state-of-the-art deep learning models. Selecting the right tool ensures efficient text processing and improves the overall performance of NLP applications.

Review Questions

1. What is tokenization and why is it important in NLP?
2. What are the three main types of tokenization? Give examples.
3. What challenges arise in word and sentence tokenization?
4. How do BPE and WordPiece handle rare or new words?
5. Compare NLTK, spaCy, and Hugging Face Tokenizers.
6. Which tokenization method would you use for sentiment analysis, and why?

2-3 Stopword Removal

Learning Outcomes

2-3-1 Define stop words and explain their role in text analysis.

2-3-2 Understand when and why stop words are removed in NLP tasks.

2-3-3 Identify common tools and libraries that provide stop word lists.

2-3-4 Evaluate when to keep or remove stop words depending on the task.

2-3-5 Customize stop word lists for specific NLP applications.

What are stop words?

Stop words are commonly used words in a language that often do not carry significant meaning in text analysis. These include words such as "the," "is," "in," "and," and "of." While these words are essential for constructing grammatically correct sentences, they are often removed in Natural Language Processing (NLP) tasks to enhance efficiency and focus on more meaningful words. The process of stop word removal helps streamline text analysis by reducing the volume of data while keeping the core information necessary for understanding the text.

The Role of Stop words in NLP Tasks

Stop words play a crucial role in text processing, as they contribute to sentence structure but often do not add informational value. In NLP applications, such as text classification, sentiment analysis, and information retrieval, removing stop words can improve computational efficiency and model performance by cutting redundant elements. Without stop word removal, models may waste processing power analyzing frequently but uninformative words, leading to increased complexity without a corresponding improvement in accuracy. However, in certain NLP tasks, stop words provide essential context, making it necessary to keep them. For example, in sentiment analysis, words like "not" or "never" are crucial in deciding the polarity of a sentence. Removing such words could alter the meaning entirely and lead to incorrect conclusions.

Common stop word lists

NLP libraries provide predefined stop word lists for different languages, making it easier for developers and researchers to incorporate stop word removal into their text preprocessing workflows. NLTK (Natural Language Toolkit) is one of the most widely used libraries for NLP and includes comprehensive stop word lists for various languages. spaCy, another popular NLP library, offers built-in stop word lists optimized for practical and efficient text processing. Scikit-learn, primarily used in machine learning applications, provides stop word lists that are often applied in text vectorization techniques. Additionally, Hugging Face Tokenizers, which supports transformer-based models, includes customizable stop word lists tailored for deep learning applications. These libraries also allow for customization, enabling users to modify stop word lists based on their specific needs by adding or removing words.

33

When to Remove or Keep Stopwords

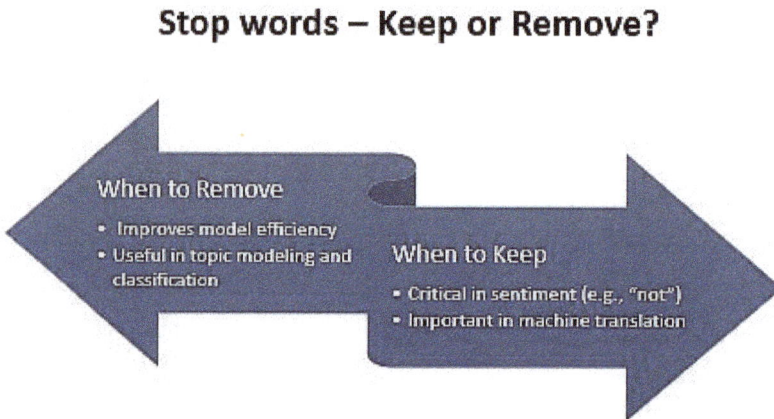

Stop words – Keep or Remove?

When to Remove
- Improves model efficiency
- Useful in topic modeling and classification

When to Keep
- Critical in sentiment (e.g., "not")
- Important in machine translation

The decision to remove or retain stop words depends on the specific NLP application and the aims of the analysis. Often removing stop words can significantly improve performance, however sometimes keeping them is necessary to preserve meaning and context.

Stopwords are often removed in text classification tasks, where dropping uninformative words help improve the relevance of features used in machine learning models. Similarly, in search engine indexing, removing stop words reduces the search space and enhances retrieval efficiency by focusing on key terms rather than common filler words. Topic modeling also receives help from stop word removal, as eliminating often occurring but insignificant words ensure that the model identifies the main subjects of the text rather than being influenced by commonly used words.

On the other hand, certain NLP tasks require the retention of stop words to ensure correct results. In machine translation, stop words play an essential role in preserving the grammatical structure of a sentence, making their removal undesirable. In question-answering systems, keeping stop words helps the model understand the meaning of user queries more effectively. Additionally, in sentiment analysis, stop words such as "not" and "never" are critical for deciding the true sentiment of a sentence. Removing them could completely change the meaning, leading to misinterpretation of emotions and inaccurate predictions.

For example, imagine you're building a search engine for a recipe website. If someone types "how to cook rice in a pot," most of those words are common stop words. You might remove them and search only for "cook rice pot" to get better results. In this case, removing stop words helps because it focuses on the important keywords. But now imagine you're doing sentiment analysis on product reviews. A review that says "I did not enjoy the product" has a very different meaning from "I enjoyed the product." If you remove the word "not," you completely change the meaning. So, in this case, you should keep stop words to preserve the true sentiment of the text. The decision depends on your task—removing stop words can help with clarity and efficiency, but keeping them can be crucial for understanding meaning.

Review Questions

1. What are stop words and why are they often removed in NLP?
2. Name three common NLP tasks where removing stop words is useful.
3. When might it be important to keep stop words in text processing?
4. Which libraries offer built-in stop word lists?
5. How can stop word lists be customized for specific needs?

2-4 Normalizing Words

Learning Outcomes

2-4-1 Define stemming and lemmatization.

2-4-2 Explain key differences between them.

2-4-3 Name common stemming algorithms.

2-4-4 Describe how lemmatization uses context.

2-4-5 Identify tools like NLTK and spaCy for text normalization.

Definition of Stemming and Lemmatization

Stemming and lemmatization are two fundamental techniques in Natural Language Processing (NLP) used to normalize words by reducing them to their base or root form. These techniques play a crucial role in text preprocessing, helping to reduce vocabulary size and improve the efficiency of text analysis. By converting words into their root forms, stemming and lemmatization allow NLP models to recognize variations of a word as the same entity, enhancing consistency in text data.

Stemming is the process of removing affixes from words to reduce them to their root form. This approach follows heuristic rules, often disregarding the actual meaning or grammatical correctness of the resulting word. Because of its rule-based nature, stemming may produce word forms that are not real words. Despite its simplicity and speed, stemming can sometimes lead to inaccurate results due to its lack of linguistic awareness.

Lemmatization, on the other hand, is a more advanced process that reduces words to their base or dictionary form, known as the lemma. Unlike stemming, lemmatization considers linguistic rules and the context in which a word appears, ensuring that the transformed word stays meaningful and grammatically correct. Since lemmatization relies on vocabulary and morphological analysis, it is typically more accurate than stemming but also computationally more expensive.

Both stemming and lemmatization are essential for various NLP applications, including search engines, chatbots, and machine learning models, where reducing word variations helps improve processing and analysis. The choice between these techniques depends on the specific requirements of the task, balancing between speed and accuracy in text normalization.

Differences

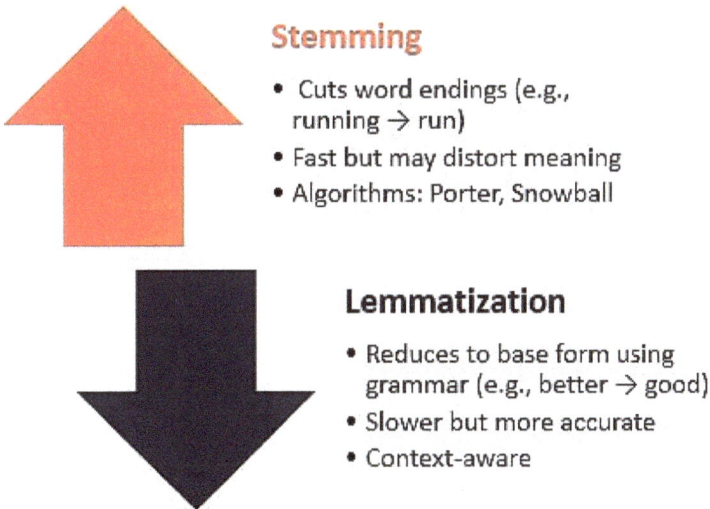

Stemming

- Cuts word endings (e.g., running → run)
- Fast but may distort meaning
- Algorithms: Porter, Snowball

Lemmatization

- Reduces to base form using grammar (e.g., better → good)
- Slower but more accurate
- Context-aware

While both stemming and lemmatization serve the purpose of reducing words to their root form, they differ in method and accuracy: Stemming is often preferred for tasks requiring speed and efficiency, while lemmatization is chosen for applications demanding linguistic accuracy.

Common Stemming Algorithms

Stemming algorithms efficiently reduce words to their root forms, each with varying levels of complexity and accuracy. These algorithms follow predefined rules to strip affixes from words, making them useful in applications where reducing word variations is necessary for text analysis. The choice of a stemming algorithm depends on the level of precision needed and the nature of the language being processed.

One of the earliest and most widely used stemming algorithms is the Porter Stemmer, developed by Martin Porter in 1980. It applies a set of heuristic rules to iteratively remove common suffixes, effectively reducing words to their base form. This algorithm is simple and efficient, making it a popular choice for NLP applications. However, due to its rule-based nature, it can sometimes produce stems that are not actual words. Despite its limitations, the Porter Stemmer stays a foundational tool in text preprocessing.

An improved version of the Porter Stemmer is the Snowball Stemmer, which offers more refined stemming and supports multiple languages. This algorithm builds upon the principles of the Porter Stemmer but enhances its accuracy by applying more sophisticated rules. It's multilingual capabilities make it a valuable tool for NLP tasks that involve processing text in different languages, providing better consistency in word normalization.

The Lancaster Stemmer, in contrast, is a much more aggressive stemming algorithm. It applies strict rules that often result in over-stemming, meaning that words are sometimes reduced to excessively simplified forms. While this can be useful in certain applications that require heavy text compression can also lead to a loss of meaning. Due to its aggressive nature, the Lancaster Stemmer is used less often when compared to the Porter and Snowball stemmers.

Each of these stemming algorithms has its advantages and drawbacks, making them suitable for different NLP tasks. While applications may receive help from the speed and simplicity of stemming, others may require more sophisticated approaches, such as lemmatization, to preserve word meanings more accurately.

For example, consider the word "connections." Using the Porter Stemmer, it would be reduced to "connect" by removing the suffix "-ions". Similarly, the Snowball Stemmer also reduces "connections" to "connect," but with slightly more refined rules that handle edge cases better in some languages. On the other hand, the Lancaster Stemmer might reduce "connections" even further to "connect" or sometimes "conn", demonstrating its more aggressive approach. These differences highlight how each algorithm handles word reduction based on its rules—Porter is lightweight and fast, Snowball is more accurate and multilingual, and Lancaster is strict but sometimes too forceful.

Lemmatization Techniques

Lemmatization is a process that relies on linguistic context and dictionaries to figure out the proper base form of a word. Unlike stemming, which simply removes affixes without considering meaning, lemmatization requires a deeper understanding of a word's part of speech (POS) to find its correct lemma. This makes lemmatization more exact and meaningful in natural language processing (NLP) applications.

One of the key techniques in lemmatization is morphological analysis, which examines the structure of words to extract their base forms. This involves breaking words down into their root components and understanding how prefixes and suffixes contribute to their overall meaning. By analyzing these patterns, lemmatization ensures that word reduction does not distort meaning.

Another essential technique is POS (part of speech) tagging, which assigns grammatical categories such as nouns, verbs, or adjectives to words. Since words can have different lemmas depending on their role in a sentence, POS tagging helps in accurately finding their base forms. For instance, the word "running" may reduce to "run" when used as a verb but might remain unchanged in other contexts.

Dictionary lookup is also a crucial part of lemmatization. Lexical databases like WordNet are often used to find the correct base form of a word by referring to comprehensive lists of lemmas. This approach ensures that words map to their most meaningful and widely recognized root forms, improving the accuracy of text analysis.

By applying these techniques, lemmatization provides a more precise method for normalizing text compared to stemming. For example, it correctly maps "running" (verb) to "run," "better" (adjective) to "good," and "children" (noun) to "child." This linguistic awareness makes lemmatization particularly valuable in applications such as search engines, text summarization, and machine translation, where preserving the correct meaning of words is essential.

For example, lemmatization reduces the word "running" to "run" when it is used as a verb, based on its part of speech. Unlike stemming, which might just chop off the "-ing" ending, lemmatization checks the grammatical role and uses a dictionary to find the proper base form. Similarly, "better" is lemmatized to "good" because it is an irregular comparative adjective, and "children" becomes "child" as the plural form of a noun. These examples show how lemmatization preserves meaning by considering context, grammar, and correct dictionary forms.

Tools for Stemming and Lemmatization

Available natural language processing (NLP) libraries provide efficient tools for performing stemming and lemmatization, making text preprocessing more effective and accessible. These tools help standardize words by reducing them to their root or base forms, which is essential for various NLP applications such as text classification, information retrieval, and machine learning.

One of the most widely used libraries for stemming and lemmatization is the Natural Language Toolkit (NLTK). NLTK offers implementations of popular stemming algorithms, such as the Porter Stemmer and Lancaster Stemmer, which help reduce words to their root forms. It also includes lemmatization capabilities through the WordNetLemmatizer, which relies on linguistic dictionaries to find the correct base form of a word. NLTK's integration with WordNet allows for more correct lemmatization by considering a word's part of speech, ensuring that words like "running" are correctly mapped to "run" when used as a verb.

Another powerful NLP library is spaCy, known for its speed and efficiency. Unlike traditional rule-based stemmers, spaCy provides an advanced lemmatization tool that is integrated into its NLP pipeline. It automatically analyzes text and assigns grammatical categories, ensuring accurate lemmatization. SpaCy's pre-trained models support multiple languages, making it a preferred choice for large-scale text processing tasks.

WordNet, a lexical database for the English language, is also commonly used for advanced lemmatization. It provides extensive information about word meanings, synonyms, and antonyms, allowing for more context-aware word transformations. By using WordNet, NLP models can improve word sense disambiguation and ensure that words are mapped to their correct root forms based on meaning rather than just heuristic rules.

Review Questions

1. What is the main goal of stemming and lemmatization?
2. How does stemming differ from lemmatization?
3. Why can stemming sometimes lead to inaccurate results?
4. What does lemmatization consider that stemming does not?
5. Which technique is more computationally expensive: stemming or lemmatization?
6. Name one common stemming algorithm.
7. What is the difference between the Porter Stemmer and the Snowball Stemmer?
8. Which stemming algorithm is known for being more aggressive?
9. What is part-of-speech (POS) tagging used for in lemmatization?
10. Which library is commonly used for both stemming and lemmatization?

2-5 Regex for Text Cleaning

Learning Outcomes

2-5-1 Describe what regular expressions (regex) are and how they are used in text cleaning.

2-5-2 Identify common text-cleaning tasks that can be performed using regex.

2-5-3 Explain how regex helps extract structured information from unstructured text.

2-5-4 Discuss how regex can standardize text formatting.

Introduction

In the world of text processing and natural language processing (NLP), regular expressions (regex) serve as a powerful tool for handling, cleaning, and manipulating textual data. Regex is a sequence of characters that define a search pattern, enabling users to match, extract or replace specific parts of text efficiently. It is widely used in various applications, including data preprocessing, information retrieval, text mining, and pattern recognition.

One of the biggest challenges in working with text data is its unstructured nature. Raw text data often has unwanted elements such as special characters, extra spaces, misspellings, and inconsistencies in formatting. These issues can hinder text analysis and machine learning models, making it essential to clean and preprocess the data before further processing. Regular expressions offer systematic and efficient approach to text cleaning, allowing users to automate complex text manipulations with minimal effort.

Common Text Cleaning Tasks

Text cleaning is an essential step in preparing data for natural language processing (NLP) tasks, as unstructured text often has noise that can negatively affect analysis. Regular expressions (regex) offer an efficient way to clean and standardize text, ensuring consistency and improving data quality. Common text-cleaning tasks using regex include removing special characters, extracting specific patterns, and replacing unwanted text.

One of the most frequent text-cleaning tasks is removing special characters and punctuation. Text datasets include symbols, punctuation marks, and other non-alphanumeric characters that may not contribute meaningful information for tasks like sentiment analysis or text classification. Cleaning the text by dropping these elements helps create a more structured dataset. For example, in cases where only letters and numbers are needed, regex can remove unwanted characters while preserving spaces to support readability. This is particularly useful for tokenization and other preprocessing steps in NLP pipelines.

For example, consider the sentence: "Wow!!! This product is amazing :)

loveit". After removing special characters and punctuation, it becomes "Wow This product is amazing loveit". Using regular expressions (regex), symbols are stripped out, leaving only the words and spaces. This cleaned version is easier to process for tasks like sentiment analysis, where emotional tone is derived more reliably from the core words rather than noisy punctuation.

Another valuable application of regex is extracting specific patterns from text. In NLP applications, structured information can be embedded within unstructured text, making it necessary to find and extract key elements. For example, regex can be used to detect email addresses within a document, ensuring that only valid formats are captured for data validation. Similarly, phone numbers appearing in various formats can be standardized by applying regex patterns that recognize different formatting conventions. Date and time-stamp extraction is also common use case, allowing log files, reports, and other time-sensitive documents to be processed efficiently. By using regex for pattern extraction, structured data can be retrieved from raw text without manual intervention.

For example, consider the sentence: "Please contact us at support@exampl e.com or call (123) 456-7890 by 05/11/2025." Using regex, we can extract the email address (support@example.com) with a pattern, the phone number ((123) 456-7890) with a pattern , and the date (05/11/2025) with a pattern. These regex patterns allow us to automatically pull structured data from unstructured text, making them extremely useful for data extraction tasks in NLP workflows.

In addition to extracting information, regex is useful for replacing or standardizing text elements. One common issue in text data is inconsistent spacing, where multiple consecutive spaces appear due to formatting errors or irregular user input. Regex can be applied to replace these unnecessary spaces with a single space, ensuring a more uniform text structure. Similarly, removing or replacing URLs in text documents is often necessary, especially in tasks such as content filtering, data anonymization, or web scraping. Regex allows users to find different URL formats and either drop them or replace them with placeholders.

By using regex for text cleaning, NLP practitioners can efficiently preprocess data, remove inconsistencies, and extract relevant information. These techniques contribute to the accuracy and reliability of text analysis, making regex a fundamental tool in natural language processing workflows.

Tools for Working with Regex

Regular expressions (regex) are widely supported across various programming languages and tools, making them an essential technique for text processing in natural language processing (NLP). They offer a powerful way to search, manipulate, and extract patterns from text, helping with tasks such as tokenization, data cleaning, and feature extraction.

One of the most used tools for regex-based text processing is Python's built-in regex module. It offers a range of functions for searching and changing text based on specific patterns. With regex, users can extract relevant information, search for specific words or phrases, and replace unwanted characters or patterns. This makes regex an invaluable tool for handling unstructured text data in NLP applications, such as removing special characters, extracting email addresses, or standardizing text formats.

Beyond Python's core functionality, NLP libraries integrate regex capabilities to enhance text preprocessing. spaCy, a widely used NLP framework, supports regex-based token matching and rule-based text processing, allowing users to define specific patterns for extracting or changing words and phrases. Similarly, NLTK (Natural Language Toolkit) includes built-in tools for regex-based text tokenization, enabling efficient segmentation of text into meaningful components. Additionally, pandas, a data analysis library, incorporates regex functionalities to manipulate text within large datasets, making it easier to filter, search, and clean textual information.

These tools make regex accessible and seamlessly integrate into broader NLP workflows. By using regex within these libraries, practitioners can efficiently preprocess text data, improve text analysis accuracy, and enhance the overall performance of NLP models.

Review Questions

1. What is the role of regex in text cleaning for NLP?
2. How does regex clean text?
3. How can regex extract specific information, such as emails or dates?
4. Why is standardizing text important in preprocessing?
5. How do NLP libraries use regex?

Chapter 3

Text Representation

3-1 Need for Text Vectorization

Learning Outcomes

3-1-1 Say what text vectorization means and why we use it.

3-1-2 Understand why computers need numbers (not words) to work with text.

3-1-3 Know some problems that come up when turning text into numbers.

3-1-4 See how vectorization helps with things like spam filters, chatbots, and translation tools.

3-1-5 Tell the difference between ways to turn words into numbers, like one-hot encoding or word embeddings.

3-1-6 Understand why word meaning and language differences matter when vectorizing text.

What is Text Vectorization?

Text vectorization is the process of converting words or sentences into numbers so that a computer can understand and analyze them. Since computers cannot directly interpret text like humans do, we need to turn text into a format they can work with, which is usually a set of numbers.

For example, imagine the sentence: "The cat sleeps."

After vectorization, the computer might turn it into something like:

The: [1, 0, 0]

Cat: [0, 1, 0]

Sleeps: [0, 0, 1]

Each word is now represented by numbers (or a "vector").

Vectorization allows a computer to process and compare words, even though the words themselves are not in their original form anymore. This way, computers can use numbers to understand the meaning of the text and perform tasks like classifying whether an email is spam or analyzing a review's sentiment.

Text Vectorization

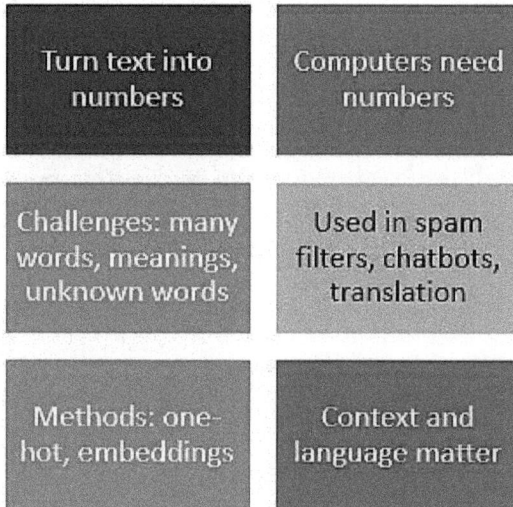

Turn text into numbers	Computers need numbers
Challenges: many words, meanings, unknown words	Used in spam filters, chatbots, translation
Methods: one-hot, embeddings	Context and language matter

Computers Need Numerical Representations

Text is one of the most abundant forms of data available in the digital world. From emails and social media posts to books, news articles, and customer reviews, a vast amount of information is stored and communicated through textual data. However, unlike humans, machines cannot inherently understand text in its raw form. Computers and machine learning models run on numerical data, which means that textual information needs to be converted into a numerical representation before it can be processed effectively.

This necessity arises because machine learning algorithms find patterns, make predictions, and extract meaningful insights based on mathematical computations. Since text is inherently unstructured, transforming it into a structured numerical format is essential for enabling algorithms to use it. The process of converting text into numerical representations is known as text vectorization. By representing words, phrases, and documents as numerical vectors, machine learning models can analyze text data, recognize relationships, and generate predictions based on linguistic patterns.

Text vectorization is a crucial step in various natural language processing (NLP) applications, such as sentiment analysis, machine translation, document classification, and chatbots. Without numerical representations of text, it would be impossible for algorithms to perform fundamental NLP tasks like word similarity comparisons, sentiment scoring, or language modeling.

Challenges in Representing Text

While text vectorization is essential, representing text numerically presents challenges. Unlike numerical data, which follows a clear mathematical structure, textual data is complex, ambiguous, and context dependent. Challenges in text representation for machine learning models include:

1. High Dimensionality

Language is rich and diverse, with thousands of words and phrases that can be combined in countless ways. Traditional text representation techniques, such as the bag-of-words model, often result in extremely high-dimensional feature spaces. For example, if a corpus (group of text documents) has 100,000 unique words, then each text document may be represented as a vector with 100,000 dimensions (columns). This high dimensionality can lead to computational inefficiencies and memory constraints, making it challenging to process large datasets.

2. Context and Meaning

Words can have multiple meanings depending on the context in which they appear. For instance, the word "bank" could refer to financial institution or the side of a river. Traditional text vectorization techniques, such as one-hot encoding, do not capture the semantic meaning of words, treating them as independent entities without considering their relationships in different contexts. More advanced techniques, such as word embeddings, address this issue by mapping words into a continuous vector space where similar words have similar numerical representations.

3. Handling Out-of-Vocabulary (OOV) Words

Text representation models rely on a predefined vocabulary of words. However, when a model encounters a word that was not seen during training (an out-of-vocabulary word), it struggles to represent it numerically. This limitation is especially problematic in real-world applications where novel words, slang, or domain-specific terms often appear. Modern approaches, such as subword embeddings (e.g., FastText), help mitigate this issue by representing words as combinations of smaller units (subwords).

4. Computational Complexity

Text representation techniques, such as deep learning-based embeddings, require extensive computational resources to train and fine-tune. Training high-quality word embeddings or language models on large corpora demand significant processing power and storage, which can be a limitation for organizations with limited resources. Additionally, complex text representations may slow down model inference, making them impractical for real-time applications.

5. Language Variability and Tokenization

Different languages have unique structures, word orders, and grammar rules that influence how text is represented. Tokenization, or breaking text into individual components (words, phrases, or subwords), is a crucial preprocessing step in text vectorization. However, tokenization techniques vary across languages, and choosing the right approach can significantly affects the performance of NLP models. For example, languages like Chinese and Japanese do not use spaces between words, making tokenization more challenging than in English.

Role of Vectorization in NLP Tasks

Text vectorization plays a fundamental role in various NLP tasks by enabling machines to process and analyze textual data efficiently. By converting text into numerical representations, vectorization allows machine learning models to find relationships between words, capture semantic meaning and perform various linguistic computations. Key applications of text vectorization in NLP include:

1. Text Classification

Text classification tasks, such as spam detection, sentiment analysis, and topic categorization, require converting text into numerical features that machine learning models can interpret. By representing documents as vectors, classification algorithms can learn patterns in the data and categorize new text instances accordingly. For example, a sentiment analysis model may classify a product review as positive or negative based on the vectorized representation of its words.

2. Information Retrieval and Search Engines

Search engines and recommendation systems rely heavily on text vectorization to index and retrieve relevant documents. By representing text as vectors, search engines can compare the similarity between user queries and indexed documents, ranking results based on relevance. Techniques such as TF-IDF (Term Frequency-Inverse Document Frequency) and word embeddings help improve the accuracy of search results by considering word importance and semantic relationships.

For example, when a user enters the query "best restaurants in New York" into a search engine, the query is first converted into a vector representation using techniques like TF-IDF or word embeddings. Each word in the query is assigned a weight based on its frequency in the user's query and its rarity across the entire document collection. The search engine then compares this vector to vectors representing the documents in its index. For instance, a document with the phrase "top-rated restaurants in New York" might have a high similarity score with the query vector due to shared terms like "restaurants" and "New York." By ranking the results based on these vector comparisons, the search engine can return the most relevant documents, improving the accuracy of the search experience.

3. Machine Translation

Vectorized text representations are essential for machine translation systems, such as Google Translate, which convert text from one language to another. Neural machine translation (NMT) models use advanced vectorization techniques, such as word embedding and transformer-based representations, to capture the contextual meaning of words and generate correct translations.

For example, in a neural machine translation system like Google Translate, the English sentence "I am going to school" is first converted into a sequence of word vectors that represent each word's meaning in context. These vectors are then processed by a transformer model, which understands word relationships and sentence structure. The model generates a translated vector sequence, which is decoded into the target language, such as French: "Je vais à l'école." The use of contextual embedding ensures that the translation reflects the correct meaning of "going to" in this context, rather than interpreting it literally or word-by-word.

4. Named Entity NER systems

NER systems find and classify entities such as names, locations, and organizations within text. Vectorization enables NER models to learn patterns in textual data, distinguishing between types of named entities. Pretrained embeddings, such as BERT (Bidirectional Encoder Representations from Transformers), have significantly improved the performance of NER systems by capturing contextual word meanings.

5. Chatbots and Conversational AI

Text vectorization is crucial in chatbot development, enabling AI models to understand and respond to user inputs meaningfully. By representing user queries as vectors, chatbot algorithms can retrieve relevant responses, generate replies, and keep context in conversations. Transformer-based models, such as GPT (Generative Pre-trained Transformer), use sophisticated vectorization techniques to generate human-like text responses.

Text Representation Techniques

The most used text vectorization techniques include:

1. One-Hot Encoding

One-hot encoding represents words as binary vectors where each unique word is assigned a position in a high-dimensional space. While simple, this method does not capture semantic relationships between words and suffers from high dimensionality.

For example, consider the vocabulary of three words: "apple," "banana," and "cherry." In a one-hot encoding scheme, each word is represented as a binary vector with a length equal to the size of the vocabulary. The word "apple" might be represented as [1, 0, 0], "banana" as [0, 1, 0], and "cherry" as [0, 0, 1]. While this method is simple and ensures that each word has a unique vector, it does not capture any semantic relationships between the words, such as the similarity between "apple" and "banana." Additionally, as the vocabulary grows, the vectors become increasingly sparse and high-dimensional, leading to inefficiencies in computation and storage.

2. Bag-of-Words (BoW)

The BoW model represents text as a frequency-based vector, counting the occurrences of words in a document. While effective for basic text classification tasks, it ignores word order and context, limiting its ability to capture meaning.

3. TF-IDF

TF-IDF (Term Frequency-Inverse Document Frequency) improves upon BoW by weighting words based on their importance in a document relative to the entire corpus. It is commonly used in information retrieval and search engines.

4. Word Embeddings

Word embeddings (Word2Vec, GloVe, FastText) map words into a continuous vector space where similar words have similar representations. Unlike earlier methods, embeddings capture semantic meaning and word relationships, improving performance in NLP tasks.

5. Transformer-Based Representations

Modern NLP models use deep learning-based embeddings generated by transformers, such as BERT and GPT. These models consider word context dynamically, producing state-of-the-art results in various NLP applications.

Review Questions

1. What is text vectorization?
2. Why do computers need numbers to understand text?
3. Give a simple example of vectorizing a sentence.
4. Name one challenge of turning text into numbers.
5. Why is word meaning hard for computers?
6. What are out-of-vocabulary words?
7. What is tokenization?
8. How does vectorization help in chatbots or sentiment analysis?
9. How is one-hot encoding different from word embeddings?
10. Which method best captures word meaning in context?

3-2 Bag of Words Model

Learning Outcomes

3-2-1 Describe how the Bag of Words (BoW) model works.

3-2-2 Explain how text is tokenized, how vocabulary is built, and how vectorization is done in BoW.

3-2-3 Distinguish between sparse and dense text representations.

3-2-4 Identify the limitations of BoW, such as ignoring word order and lacking semantic understanding.

3-2-5 Recognize situations where BoW may be appropriate or insufficient for NLP tasks.

Concept of BoW Representation

The Bag of Words (BoW) model is one of the most fundamental techniques for text vectorization in natural language processing (NLP). It is widely used to convert text into numerical representations that machine learning algorithms can process. The BoW model represents a document as an unordered collection (or "bag") of words while disregarding grammar, word order, and sentence structure. Instead of preserving the sequence of words, it focuses on their frequency within a document.

BoW is a simple yet effective technique for NLP tasks, including document classification, sentiment analysis, and information retrieval. Despite its simplicity, the model has significant applications and is still a foundational approach in text processing. By breaking text into individual words and counting their occurrences, BoW offers a structured way to analyze textual data numerically. However, because it does not account for contextual relationships between words, it has certain limitations.

Bag of Words (BoW)

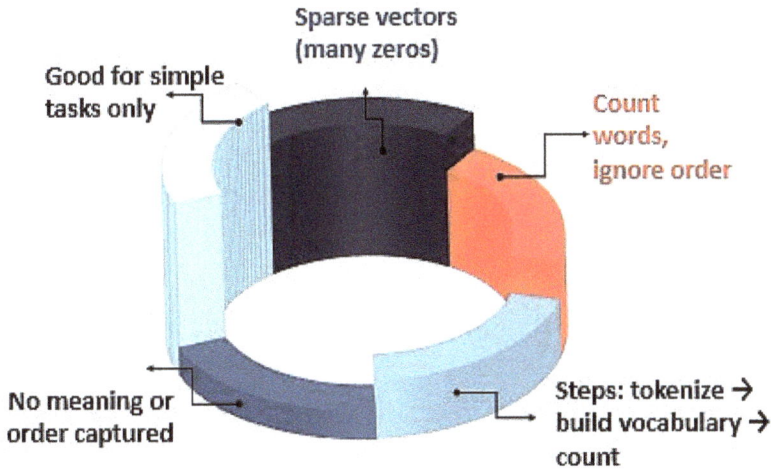

Sparse vectors
(many zeros)

Good for simple
tasks only

Count
words,
ignore order

No meaning or
order captured

Steps: tokenize →
build vocabulary →
count

How BoW Converts Text into a Numerical Format

The BoW model follows a straightforward process to transform raw text data into a format suitable for machine learning.

Tokenization is the first step in processing text data, where a sentence or document is broken down into smaller units called tokens. These tokens can be words, subwords, or characters, depending on the tokenization method used. For example, the sentence *"The cat sat on the mat."* would be tokenized into individual words: ["The", "cat", "sat", "on", "the", "mat"]. Tokenization helps in structuring textual data, making it easier for algorithms to process and analyze.

After tokenization, the next step is vocabulary construction, where a unique set of words from the entire dataset, known as a corpus, is named. This vocabulary consists of all distinct words appearing across multiple documents. For instance, if we have two sentences—*"The cat sat on the mat."* and *"The dog lay on the rug."*—the vocabulary would include the unique words: ["The", "cat", "sat", "on", "the", "mat", "dog", "lay", "rug"]. Building vocabulary is crucial because it forms the basis for representing text data numerically, allowing machine learning models to process language efficiently.

The last step in transforming text into a machine-readable format is vectorization, also known as feature extraction. In this step, each document is converted into a numerical representation based on the vocabulary. One common technique is the Bag-of-Words (BoW) model, where each word in the vocabulary is represented as a column in a matrix, and each row corresponds to a document. The value in each cell stands for the frequency of the word in that document. For example, using the vocabulary mentioned earlier, the first sentence would be represented as [1, 1, 1, 1, 1, 1, 0, 0, 0], indicating that all its words appear once, while the second sentence would be represented as [1, 0, 0, 1, 1, 0, 1, 1, 1], reflecting the presence and absence of words accordingly.

Word	The	cat	sat	on	the	mat	dog	lay	rug
Sentence 1	1	1	1	1	1	1	0	0	0
Sentence 2	1	0	0	1	1	0	1	1	1

By performing tokenization, vocabulary construction, and vectorization, textual data is transformed into a structured numerical format that can be processed by machine learning models. These steps are fundamental in natural language processing (NLP) and enable various applications such as text classification, sentiment analysis, and document clustering.

Sparse vs. Dense Representations

When text data gets converted into numerical forms using models like the Bag-of-Words (BoW) approach, it often results in high-dimensional vectors, which hold many zero values. This distinction leads to two primary types of text representations: sparse and dense.

A sparse representation occurs where a high percentage of the elements are zero. This occurs because a single document typically holds only a fraction of the total vocabulary, meaning that most words in a large corpus do not appear in each text sample. For instance, in a vocabulary of 50,000 words, a document may only use a few hundred, leading to a vector with mostly zero values. While sparse representations are straightforward to generate and interpret, they present computational challenges. They need significant storage space, increasing processing time due to high-dimensionality, and can cause inefficiencies in machine learning algorithms, as traditional models struggle with high-dimensional sparse data.

In contrast, dense representations are more compact and have mostly non-zero values. These representations appear from more advanced techniques like Word Embeddings (such as Word2Vec and GloVe) and Transformer-based models (like BERT), which capture the semantic relationships between words. Unlike BoW, which treats words as independent features, these map words into a continuous vector space where similar words have similar numerical representations. Dense representations significantly improve computational efficiency, reduce memory usage, and enhance model performance by capturing contextual meanings rather than relying solely on raw word frequency.

For example, consider the sentence "The cat sat on the mat." In a sparse representation using a Bag-of-Words model with a vocabulary of 10,000 words, the sentence might be encoded as a vector where only the positions for "the," "cat," "sat," "on," and "mat" have a value of 1, and the remaining 9,995 positions are 0. This leads to a high-dimensional, mostly-zero vector that is easy to interpret but inefficient to store and compute. In contrast, using a dense representation like Word2Vec or BERT, each word is mapped to a lower-dimensional vector (e.g., 300 dimensions for Word2Vec), where all values are real numbers and none are exactly zero. These vectors capture nuanced relationships—like the similarity between "cat" and "dog"—and are more compact, enabling faster processing and better model performance.

While the BoW model inherently produces sparse representations and is often less efficient than modern embedding techniques, it stays a valuable method for simpler NLP applications. BoW is often used as a baseline in text classification tasks, offering an interpretable and easy-to-implement approach before transitioning to more complex deep learning models.

Limitations of BoW

Despite its usefulness, the BoW model has limitations that can affect its effectiveness in NLP tasks.

1. Loss of Word Order

Since BoW considers only word frequency and ignores word sequence, it does not capture the meaning conveyed by word order. For example, the sentences:

"The dog chased the cat."

"The cat chased the dog."

Would have the same BoW representation, even though their meanings are entirely different. This limitation makes BoW less effective in applications that rely on syntactic structure, such as machine translation or question answering.

2. Large Feature Space

As the vocabulary size increases, the feature space grows significantly. In a large corpus having thousands or millions of unique words, the resulting BoW matrix can become extremely high-dimensional, making computations expensive and inefficient. This problem is especially prominent in cases where a dataset has domain-specific terms, jargon, or infrequent words.

3. Lack of Semantic Understanding

BoW treats words as independent entities and does not account for relationships between words. For instance, the words *"happy"* and *"joyful"* are considered entirely distinct, despite being semantically similar. This limitation reduces the model's ability to generalize well across different variations of text.

4. Sensitivity to Vocabulary Size and Stopwords

The presence of simple words (e.g., "the," "is," "and") can dominate the BoW representation, affecting the importance of more meaningful words. While stop word removal techniques can address this issue, they require added preprocessing steps.

Due to these limitations, BoW is often used in conjunction with other techniques, such as Term Frequency-Inverse Document Frequency (TF-IDF) or word embeddings, to improve its effectiveness.

Review Questions

1. What does the Bag of Words model ignore about text?
2. How does BoW convert sentences into numbers?
3. What is tokenization?
4. Why is the BoW vector often sparse?
5. How is a sparse vector different from a dense one?
6. What is the limitation of BoW related to word meaning?
7. What do BoW and word embeddings represent differently?
8. What kind of tasks might BoW struggle with due to loss of word order?
9. Why are stopwords a problem in BoW?

3-3 TF-IDF

Learning Outcomes

3-3-1 Know what Term Frequency (TF) means.

3-3-2 Know what Inverse Document Frequency (IDF) means.

3-3-3 Understand how TF and IDF work together in TF-IDF.

3-3-4 See how TF-IDF helps find important words in documents.

3-3-5 Compare TF-IDF with Bag of Words in simple terms.

Understanding TF-IDF

Text data is inherently unstructured and must be transformed into a numerical format before machine learning algorithms can process it. One of the most popular techniques for text vectorization is TF-IDF (Term Frequency-Inverse Document Frequency), which improves upon the traditional Bag of Words (BoW) model by accounting for the importance of words across multiple documents.

TF-IDF is a statistical measure used in Natural Language Processing (NLP) and information retrieval to evaluate how relevant a word is to a document in a collection of documents. Unlike BoW, which simply counts word occurrences, TF-IDF adjusts the frequency based on how commonly a word appears across the entire corpus. This method helps emphasize unique words while reducing the influence of often occurring but less informative words, such as "the," "is," and "and."

TF-IDF consists of two main components:

- Term Frequency (TF) – Measures how often a term appears in a document.

- Inverse Document Frequency (IDF) – Measures how important a term is by assessing how commonly it appears across all documents.

By combining these two measures, TF-IDF assigns higher weights to words that are important in a specific document while down-weighting words that appear often across all documents.

The Mathematical Formula of TF-IDF

TF-IDF (Term Frequency-Inverse Document Frequency) is a widely used statistical measure in Natural Language Processing (NLP) and information retrieval. It quantifies the importance of a word within a document while considering its overall significance across an entire corpus. The TF-IDF score is calculated as the product of two components: Term Frequency (TF) and Inverse Document Frequency (IDF).

Term Frequency (TF)

Term Frequency (TF) is how often a specific word appears within a document. It is calculated using the formula:

$$TF(t, d) = \frac{f_t}{N}$$

Where:

t is the term (word).

d is the document.

f is the number of times the term tt appears in document d.

N is the total number of words in document d.

For instance, if the word "machine" appears three times in a document having one hundred words, its term frequency would be 3% of the document's total word count. Higher TF values suggest that a word is more prominent within a specific document. However, often occurring words like "the" or "is" may have high TF values across multiple documents, reducing their significance.

Inverse Document Frequency (IDF)

Inverse Document Frequency (IDF) accounts for the importance of a term across the entire corpus. Words that are common across documents receive lower IDF scores, while rare but informative words obtain higher scores. The IDF formula is:

$$IDF(t) = \log\left(\frac{D}{1 + d_t}\right)$$

Where:

D is the total number of documents in the corpus.

d is the number of documents that hold the term t

The 1 in the denominator prevents division by zero in cases where a term is absent from all documents.

For example, if the word "machine" appears in 5 out of 1000 documents, its IDF score is calculated as:

$$IDF(\text{"machine"}) = \log\left(\frac{1000}{1+5}\right) = \log(166.67) \approx 2.22$$

This means that "machine" is not overly common in the corpus, giving it a high IDF score. Words that appear in every document, such as "the" or "and," would have much lower IDF values, reducing their overall significance.

The final TF-IDF score for a term in a document is obtained by multiplying TF and IDF:

$$TF\text{-}IDF(t, d) = TF(t, d) \times IDF(t)$$

Using the earlier values for the word "machine":

$$TF\text{-}IDF(\text{"machine"}) = 0.03 \times 2.22 = 0.0666$$

This score stands for the importance of the word "machine" in the document compared to the entire corpus. Higher TF-IDF values show words that are both frequent within a specific document and rare across the corpus, making them useful for distinguishing documents in tasks such as text classification, search engine ranking, and topic modeling.

TF-IDF balances the local importance of a term in a document with its global significance across a dataset. This ensures that often occurring, but uninformative words are down weighted, while rare and meaningful terms receive higher emphasis, making TF-IDF a fundamental technique in text analysis and information retrieval.

TF-IDF Reduces Impact of Common Words

One of the main advantages of TF-IDF is that it helps address a major weakness of the Bag of Words (BoW) model: the overrepresentation of frequent but unimportant words. In BoW, words like "the," "is," "and," or "of" tend to dominate the text representation simply because they appear often, even though they contribute little meaning. TF-IDF counters this problem by assigning lower weights to such words. For example, the word "the" may appear in every document, resulting in a low IDF score close to zero, while a more specialized word like "artificial," which appears in only a few documents, will have a higher IDF score, making it more significant in distinguishing one document from another. This ability to filter out uninformative words while emphasizing rare but meaningful terms makes TF-IDF a more refined and effective text vectorization technique compared to BoW.

Advantages of TF-IDF Over BoW

Feature	Bag of Words (BoW)	TF-IDF
Basic Idea	Counts how often each word appears in a document	Weighs words based on how important they are in a document relative to the whole corpus
Representation	Vector of raw word counts	Vector of weighted word counts reflecting term importance
Emphasis	Frequency of words only	Balances frequency with how unique the word is across documents
Handling Common Words	Treats all words equally	Downweights common words like "the", "and"
Sparsity	High sparsity due to many zero counts	Also, sparse but weights reduce impact of common words
Use Cases	Simple text classification, topic modeling	Information retrieval, text classification with better weighting
Advantages	Easy to compute and understand	Captures term importance, improves performance in many tasks
Disadvantages	Ignores word importance and context	More complex calculation, may need normalization

1. Assigns Higher Importance to Meaningful Words

Unlike BoW, which treats all words equally, TF-IDF prioritizes words that are more relevant to a document while down-weighting words that appear in multiple documents.

2. Reduces Noise from Frequent Words

Familiar words such as "the," "is," and "and" are assigned low scores, reducing their influence in the model. This improves text classification and retrieval performance.

3. More Efficient Than BoW in High-Dimensional Spaces

BoW creates large and sparse feature vectors, leading to high-dimensional datasets. TF-IDF reduces the dominance of redundant words, making computations more efficient.

4. Improves Search Engine and Information Retrieval Systems

Search engines use TF-IDF to rank documents based on keyword relevance. Since IDF reduces the impact of often occurring words, search results are more correct.

5. Preserves Distinctive Terms for Text Classification

In classification tasks such as spam detection or sentiment analysis, TF-IDF ensures that rare but meaningful words (like "fraud" in spam emails) receive higher importance, improving model performance.

Review Questions

1. What does Term Frequency (TF) measure in a document?
2. What does Inverse Document Frequency (IDF) tell us about a word?
3. How does TF-IDF combine TF and IDF to find important words?
4. Why is TF-IDF better than the Bag of Words method?
5. How does TF-IDF handle common words like "the" and "is"?
6. In your own words, explain why TF-IDF is useful in text analysis.
7. Give one example of where TF-IDF might be used in real life.
8. What kind of words get high TF-IDF scores?
9. What kind of words get low TF-IDF scores?
10. How does TF-IDF help computers understand text better?

3-4 Word Embeddings

Learning Outcomes

3-4-1 Understand what Term Frequency (TF) means.

3-4-2 Understand what Inverse Document Frequency (IDF) means.

3-4-3 Explain how TF and IDF work together in TF-IDF.

3-4-4 Describe how TF-IDF finds important words in a document.

3-4-5 Compare TF-IDF to the Bag of Words method.

Distributed Word Representations

Traditional text representation techniques, such as the Bag of Words (BoW) and TF-IDF, treat words as independent entities without capturing their semantic relationships. While these methods are effective for basic text processing tasks, they do not preserve the meaning of words in context.

To address these limitations, word embeddings were introduced. Word embeddings are a type of distributed word representation, where words are mapped to dense, continuous vector spaces that encode their meanings based on context. Unlike sparse and high-dimensional BoW representations, word embeddings create compact, meaningful numerical representations where words with similar meanings have similar vector representations.

By using large-scale corpora and unsupervised learning techniques, word embeddings capture complex linguistic relationships, such as synonymy, analogy, and semantic similarity. Popular word embedding models include Word2Vec, GloVe, and FastText, each offering unique approaches to learning word representations.

Word2Vec

Skip-gram vs. Continuous Bag of Words

Word2Vec, developed by researchers at Google, is one of the most influential word embedding techniques, transforming words into dense vectors by analyzing their surrounding words in large text corpora. It uses through two primary architectures: Continuous Bag of Words (CBOW) and the Skip-gram model. CBOW predicts a target word based on its surrounding context words, making it efficient for large datasets and faster than the Skip-gram model. For example, given the context words ["The", "dog", "on", "the"], CBOW predicts the missing word "sat." In contrast, the Skip-gram model works in the opposite way by predicting surrounding context words based on a given target word. This approach performs well even with limited data and captures rare words effectively. For instance, if given the word "sat," the model predicts words like ["The", "dog", "on", "the"]. The key distinction between CBOW and Skip-gram lies in their learning approach: CBOW focuses on predicting a central word using context, while Skip-gram learns to predict context words based on a target word.

Word2Vec Captures Semantic Relationships

A major strength of Word2Vec is its ability to capture semantic relationships between words through vector arithmetic. Because words with similar meanings are positioned closer together in the vector space, the model can find relationships and solve analogy-based queries. For example, if the vector representation of "king" is adjusted by subtracting "man" and adding "woman," the result is a vector representation close to "queen." This capability enables Word2Vec to model linguistic relationships such as synonyms, antonyms, and word analogies, making it a valuable tool for various natural language processing applications.

GloVe

Co-occurrence Matrix-Based Word Embeddings

Unlike Word2Vec, which relies on local context windows, GloVe (Global Vectors for Word Representation) is based on word co-occurrence matrices. Developed by researchers at Stanford, GloVe constructs word vectors by analyzing the frequency with which words appear together across an entire corpus.

A co-occurrence matrix is a table that records how often words appear together in each window size. For example, if the words "cat" and "dog" often appear in similar contexts, their vectors will be closer in space. GloVe learns these relationships by factorizing the co-occurrence matrix and improving word vectors such that the dot product of two-word vectors approximates their probability of co-occurrence.

How GloVe Differs from Word2Vec

GloVe is particularly useful for capturing global corpus-wide statistics, making it ideal for applications like document similarity, information retrieval, and knowledge graph construction.

FastText

FastText, developed by Facebook AI, improves upon traditional word embedding techniques like Word2Vec and GloVe by addressing the limitations associated with rare words and out-of-vocabulary (OOV) words. Unlike these earlier models, which treat words as single atomic units, FastText represents words as subword units, specifically character n-grams. Instead of learning a single vector for each word, the model learns embeddings for smaller components of words and then combines them to form a complete word representation.

Subword Representation

One of the key innovations of FastText is its ability to break words down into overlapping subword components. For example, the word "playing" is decomposed into multiple n-grams such as "play," "lay," "ying," and "ing." This approach allows FastText to recognize morphological relationships between words more effectively than models that rely solely on whole-word embeddings. Words with similar roots, such as "play" and "playing," will have overlapping subwords, helping the model set up meaningful connections between them.

Spelling Variations and Rare Words

A significant advantage of FastText is its ability to handle spelling variations and regional differences in word usage. For instance, the words "color" and "colour" remain similar in FastText's vector space because they share common subword components. Additionally, this approach helps manage misspellings, allowing the model to understand that "recieve" and "receive" are closely related, even though one is an incorrect spelling.

FastText is also highly effective in representing rare words. Traditional word embedding models struggle with words that appear infrequently in the training corpus, as they lack sufficient context to generate meaningful representations. However, since FastText constructs words from smaller, known subword components, even an unfamiliar word can still be represented based on its constituent parts. This feature makes FastText particularly useful in languages with rich morphology, where words often include multiple prefixes and suffixes that change their meaning.

Advantages of FastText

By incorporating subword information, FastText provides a more flexible and robust approach to word embeddings. It enhances the representation of rare words, accounts for spelling variations, and captures finer-grained linguistic relationships. These capabilities make FastText an essential tool in natural language processing tasks such as text classification, machine translation, and sentiment analysis. Additionally, its ability to model word similarities at a more granular level improves overall language understanding in computational systems.

FastText builds upon and surpasses traditional word embedding techniques by leveraging subword units, making it an indispensable resource for modern NLP applications. Its ability to handle rare words, spelling inconsistencies, and complex linguistic structures make it particularly valuable for languages with high morphological complexity.

Review Questions

1. Why are traditional methods like Bag of Words (BoW) and TF-IDF limited when representing word meaning?
2. What are word embeddings, and how do they improve upon traditional text representations?
3. How do Word2Vec, GloVe, and FastText differ in the way they learn word meanings?
4. Why is FastText especially useful for handling rare words, spelling variations, and morphologically complex languages?

3-5 Contextual Embeddings

Learning Outcomes

3-5-1 Identify limitations of traditional word embeddings.

3-5-2 Explain how ELMo and BERT generate context-based word meanings.

3-5-3 Describe how BERT and Transformers improve NLP tasks.

3-5-4 Give examples of tasks that benefit from contextual embeddings.

Traditional word embeddings, such as Word2Vec and GloVe, assign a single static vector to each word, which does not account for polysemy and contextual variations in meaning. Contextual embeddings address these limitations by dynamically generating word representations based on the surrounding text. Two influential models in this space are ELMo and BERT, both of which use deep learning architectures to provide more accurate and flexible word embedding.

ELMo: Contextualized Word Representations

ELMo (Embeddings from Language Models), developed by the Allen Institute for AI, is a significant advancement in word embedding techniques. Unlike traditional models that assign a fixed vector to each word, ELMo creates dynamic embeddings by analyzing entire sentences. It uses bidirectional Long Short-Term Memory (LSTM) networks, allowing it to consider both preceding and following words when deciding the meaning of a given word.

For example, the word "bank" has different meanings in the sentences "He went to the bank to withdraw money" and "The boat was tied to the riverbank." Traditional embeddings would assign the same vector to "bank" in both contexts, but ELMo generates distinct representations based on the surrounding words. This context-aware approach makes ELMo particularly effective for tasks such as named entity recognition, coreference resolution, and sentiment analysis, where understanding word meaning in different contexts is crucial.

BERT: Bidirectional Contextual Understanding

BERT (Bidirectional Encoder Representations from Transformers), developed by Google, is a breakthrough in NLP by introducing true bidirectional context awareness. Prior models processed text either left-to-right (as in traditional language models) or right-to-left (as in RNN-based approaches), limiting their ability to fully capture context. BERT overcomes this by analyzing words in both directions simultaneously using the Transformer architecture.

One of BERT's key advantages is its ability to deeply understand contextual meaning by considering the entire sentence at once. This enables it to outperform earlier models on a wide range of NLP tasks, including question answering, text summarization, and named entity recognition. Another major strength of BERT is its flexibility—it can be fine-tuned for specific applications, allowing it to adapt to various domains and datasets with minimal added training. This adaptability has made BERT a foundational model in modern NLP research and applications.

Transformers: The Future of NLP

The Transformer architecture, introduced in the paper *Attention Is All You Need*, forms the basis of BERT and other state-of-the-art NLP models, including GPT (Generative Pre-trained Transformer) and T5 (Text-to-Text Transfer Transformer). Transformers improve upon earlier sequential models, such as LSTMs and RNNs, by using self-attention mechanisms, which allow them to process entire text sequences in parallel rather than one word at a time.

This not only speeds up training but also enables Transformers to capture long-range dependencies in text more effectively. As a result, Transformer-based models have set new benchmarks across a wide array of NLP tasks, from language translation to text generation. Their scalability and efficiency have solidified their place as the foundation of modern NLP, shaping the future of AI-driven language understanding.

Review Questions

1. What is a key limitation of traditional word embeddings like Word2Vec?
2. How does ELMo handle word meaning differently from traditional embeddings?
3. What makes BERT's approach to context unique?
4. Why are Transformers important in models like BERT and GPT?
5. Name one NLP task that improves with contextual embeddings and explains why.

Chapter 4

Sentiment Analysis

4-1 Understanding Sentiment in Text

Learning Outcomes

4-1-1 Define sentiment analysis and its role in NLP.

4-1-2 List common uses of sentiment analysis in real life.

4-1-3 Identify and compare types of sentiment analysis.

4-1-4 Describe key challenges in sentiment detection.

4-1-5 Explain how context, negation, and emotion affect sentiment.

Definition

Sentiment analysis, also known as opinion mining, is a field of Natural Language Processing (NLP) that involves figuring out the emotional tone, attitude, or subjective information in each text. This process allows machines to analyze opinions, emotions, and sentiments expressed in written language. By using sentiment analysis, businesses, researchers, and developers can gain insights into customer feedback, social media trends, and public opinion.

Why Sentiment Analysis is Important

Sentiment analysis plays a crucial role in NLP because it helps in understanding human emotions and opinions at scale. It is widely used in industries such as marketing, finance, healthcare, and politics to analyze customer feedback, check brand reputation, and assess market trends. By automating sentiment classification, businesses can efficiently process large volumes of text data, leading to improved decision-making and customer engagement. Additionally, sentiment analysis enhances chatbot interactions, content moderation, and personalized recommendations in various AI-driven applications.

Types of Sentiment Analysis

Sentiment analysis methods are based on the level of granularity and the nature of sentiment detection.

Binary Sentiment Classification

This is the simplest form of sentiment analysis, where information is classified into two categories: positive or negative. It is commonly used for product reviews, social media analysis, and customer feedback to decide whether a sentiment is favorable or unfavorable.

Multi-class Sentiment Classification

In this approach, sentiment is classified into three categories: positive, neutral, or negative. This method provides a more refined understanding of sentiment, allowing for the inclusion of neutral opinions that do not strongly lean toward either positivity or negativity.

Fine-Grained Sentiment Classification

Fine-grained sentiment analysis assigns sentiment scores on a more detailed scale, such as rating reviews on a 1-to-5-star system. This approach enables businesses to differentiate between varying degrees of satisfaction or dissatisfaction, offering deeper insights into customer sentiment.

Aspect-Based Sentiment Analysis

Aspect-based sentiment analysis (ABSA) goes beyond overall sentiment classification by finding specific aspects or features of a product or service that users mention in their reviews. For example, in a restaurant review, ABSA can figure out whether the user expresses positive sentiment about the food but negative sentiment about the service.

Emotion Detection

Emotion detection sentiment analysis categorizes text based on emotions such as joy, anger, sadness, fear, or surprise. This approach is valuable for understanding customer emotions in social media monitoring, psychological studies, and personalized content recommendations.

Challenges in Sentiment Analysis

Sentiment analysis faces challenges that change its accuracy and effectiveness.

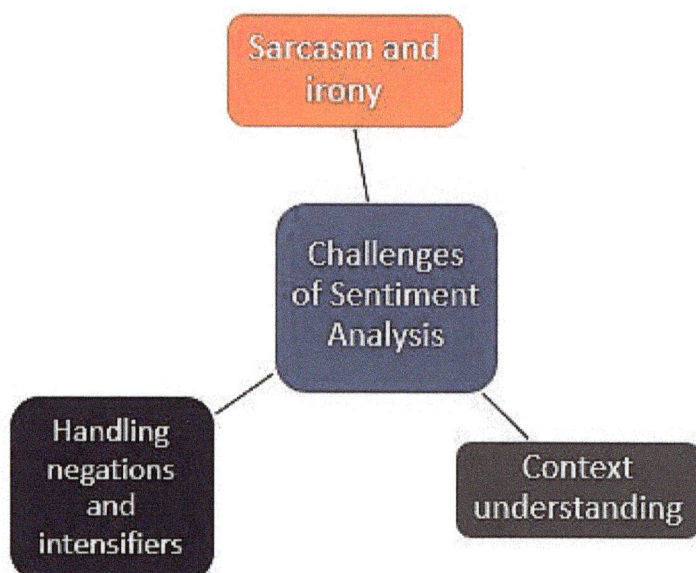

Sarcasm and Irony Detection

One of the most significant challenges in sentiment analysis is detecting sarcasm and irony. Sarcastic statements often express the opposite of their literal meaning, making it difficult for NLP models to correctly interpret sentiment. For example, the phrase "Oh great, another delay!" is negative despite the presence of the word "great."

Contextual Understanding

Understanding sentiment requires considering the context in which words are used. The same word can convey different sentiments based on its surrounding words. For instance, the word "cold" in "cold-hearted" has a negative connotation, while in "cold drink," it is neutral or positive.

Handling Negations and Intensifiers

Negations (e.g., "not good") and intensifiers (e.g., "very bad") significantly change sentiment interpretation. NLP models must recognize how these linguistic elements alter the sentiment of a phrase. Without proper handling, a sentence like "This movie is not bad" might be misclassified as negative instead of neutral or slightly positive.

Review Questions

1. What is sentiment analysis?
2. Name two uses of sentiment analysis.
3. What's the difference between binary and multi-class sentiment classification?
4. What does aspect-based sentiment analysis do?
5. Why is sarcasm hard for sentiment models to detect?
6. How does context change the meaning of words in sentiment analysis?
7. What are negations and intensifiers? Give an example.

4-2 Rule-Based Sentiment Analysis

Learning Outcomes

4-2-1 Explain how rule-based sentiment analysis works.

4-2-2 Identify key sentiment lexicons (SentiWordNet, VADER, AFINN).

4-2-3 Describe the strengths and weaknesses of rule-based methods.

4-2-4 Recognize the role of rules in handling polarity, negation, and intensity.

How Rule-Based Approaches Work

Rule-based sentiment analysis is a traditional approach that finds the sentiment of a text using predefined rules, sentiment lexicons, and heuristic techniques. These methods rely on manually created dictionaries of words and phrases associated with specific sentiments, such as positive, negative, or neutral emotions. When analyzing text, the system matches words against these lexicons and calculates an overall sentiment score based on predefined rules, such as word polarity, intensity, and negation handling.

For example, if a sentence has the word "excellent," a rule-based system would recognize it as a positive sentiment. However, if the sentence includes "not excellent," more rules must be in place to correctly interpret the negation and adjust the sentiment accordingly. Rule-based methods are often used for quick and interpretable sentiment analysis, especially in domains where computational resources are limited.

Sentiment Lexicons and Dictionaries

Lexicons and dictionaries have been developed to support rule-based sentiment analysis. These lexicons have lists of words with predefined sentiment scores that guide the sentiment classification process.

SentiWordNet is an extension of WordNet that assigns sentiment scores to words based on their meaning and context. Each word has three scores: positivity, negativity, and neutrality, which can be used to figure out the sentiment of a given text. SentiWordNet is useful for understanding word-level sentiment but requires other rules to oversee negations and context.

VADER (Valence Aware Dictionary and sEntiment Reasoner) is a lexicon and rule-based sentiment analysis tool specifically designed for analyzing social media text. It accounts for text characteristics such as capital letters, punctuation (e.g., "!!!"), and emoticons to improve sentiment detection. Unlike traditional lexicons, VADER also considers the intensity of words, making it effective for short, informal text, including tweets and reviews.

AFINN is another lexicon-based sentiment dictionary that assigns integer sentiment scores to words. It is widely used for sentiment analysis tasks where words are mapped to a scale of negativity or positivity. The simplicity of AFINN makes it useful for quick sentiment classification, though it may struggle with context and nuanced language.

Pros and Cons of Rule-Based Sentiment Analysis

Rule-based sentiment analysis is a clear and accessible way to gauge emotion in text, often chosen for its simplicity and transparency. One of its key strengths is how fast and lightweight it is—it doesn't demand much processing power compared to machine learning models. Because it relies on established rules and word lists, it's also easy to interpret; users can trace exactly how a sentiment score was determined. Another advantage is that it doesn't depend on pre-labeled training data, making it ideal when annotated examples are hard to come by.

That said, there are definite trade-offs. One big challenge is that rule-based systems aren't great at picking up on context. Sarcasm, idioms, and subtle language cues often go unnoticed because the system interprets text based on fixed rules. It can also fall behind when it comes to newer slang or specialized vocabulary in certain fields. Another common issue is handling negation and intensity. Expressions like "not terrible" or "extremely happy" need more nuanced rules to interpret correctly, which can make the setup more complicated than it first appears. Still, for straightforward sentiment tasks where speed and explainability matter more than nuance, rule-based methods remain a practical choice.

Example

The bakery had received dozens of short reviews through social media and their website. The owner, curious to know whether the overall sentiment leaned positive or negative, asked for help interpreting the feedback. Instead of diving into complex models that require large amounts of training data, we opted for a rule-based method: a straightforward system that relies on predefined word lists and a simple scoring system.

The process began with cleaning the text. Each review was converted to lowercase, punctuation was stripped away, and sentences were broken down into individual words. This step, often called preprocessing, helps ensure that the computer can analyze the text without getting distracted by irrelevant details like capitalization or commas.

Next came the creation of two lexicons: one containing positive words, such as delicious, friendly, and fresh, and another filled with negative terms like slow, rude, or stale. These lists were kept small and intuitive to reflect the simple nature of the task. The core idea was simple: for each review, we counted the number of positive and negative words. If a review contained more positive words than negative, it was labeled as "positive." If it had more negative words, it was labeled "negative." An equal number resulted in a "neutral" score.

One review, for instance, read: "The bread was fresh and delicious, but the service was slow." Here, the words fresh and delicious scored positive points, while slow counted against the total. The final score was positive, even though the review contained a complaint. This example illustrates both the strength and the weakness of rule-based systems: they are easy to understand and quick to implement, but they can miss nuance and context.

After applying this method to 50 customer reviews, the results were promising: most reviews were classified in a way that aligned with a human reader's interpretation. The majority were positive, a smaller portion negative, and a few fell into the neutral category. However, some reviews proved tricky. Sarcastic comments or phrases like "not bad" confused the system, as it lacked the ability to process context or handle negation effectively.

Despite these limitations, the rule-based method fulfilled its purpose. It provided a quick, transparent way to analyze sentiment without needing advanced tools or large datasets. For a small business or a beginner in data analysis, this approach offers an excellent starting point—a bridge between raw text and actionable insight.

While rule-based sentiment analysis lacks the subtlety of machine learning, its clarity and simplicity make it a valuable educational tool. It demonstrates the core ideas behind natural language processing in a way that is approachable, hands-on, and immediately useful.

Review Questions

1. What is rule-based sentiment analysis?
2. How does a system determine sentiment using a lexicon?
3. What makes VADER different from other sentiment lexicons?
4. Name one strength and one limitation of rule-based sentiment analysis.
5. Why is handling negation important in rule-based systems?
6. Which lexicon would be most useful for social media text, and why?

4-3 Machine Learning-Based Sentiment Analysis

Learning Outcomes
4-3-1 Understand machine learning vs. deep learning for sentiment analysis.
4-3-2 Identify key machine learning models (e.g., Logistic Regression, Naïve Bayes).
4-3-3 Explain how deep learning models (e.g., RNN, LSTM, BERT) help sentiment analysis.
4-3-4 Understand word embeddings (e.g., Word2Vec, GloVe).
4-3-5 Describe the steps to build and evaluate a sentiment analysis model.

Overview of Machine Learning Approaches

Machine learning-based sentiment analysis is a more advanced approach than rule-based methods, as it enables models to learn from data rather than relying on predefined lexicons. These models use supervised learning techniques, where they are trained on labeled datasets having text samples and their corresponding sentiment labels (e.g., positive, negative, neutral). Once trained, the model can predict sentiment for new, unseen text.

Rule-Based vs. ML-Based Sentiment Analysis

Feature	Rule-Based Sentiment Analysis	ML-Based Sentiment Analysis
Method	Uses predefined sentiment rules	Learns from labeled text data
Core Approach	Matches positive/negative words	Converts text into vectors, trains a model
Negation Handling	Handled manually	Learned through context
Scoring	Based on rule matching	Based on model predictions
Interpretability	Easy to understand	Less transparent
Flexibility	Limited adaptability	More flexible, adapts to new data
Data Requirement	No training data needed	Requires labeled training data

Machine learning approaches to sentiment analysis can be categorized into traditional machine learning models and deep learning-based models. Traditional models rely on manually engineered features, while deep learning models learn complex linguistic patterns from substantial amounts of data.

Traditional ML Models

Traditional machine learning models have long been used in sentiment classification tasks, where the goal is to find the sentiment or opinion expressed in a piece of text. These models rely on numerical representations of text, such as Bag of Words (BoW), TF-IDF (Term Frequency-Inverse Document Frequency), or word embeddings, to extract meaningful features from the text before making predictions. Different machine learning models have proven effective for sentiment analysis, each with its own strengths and applications.

One of the simplest and most widely used models in sentiment classification is Logistic Regression. This model predicts the probability that a given text belongs to a particular sentiment class, such as positive or negative. Logistic Regression is especially effective for binary sentiment classification tasks and is appreciated for its interpretability, allowing easy examination of the influence of individual features on the prediction. Its simplicity and ease of implementation make it a popular choice for text classification problems.

Another commonly used model is Naïve Bayes, a probabilistic classifier grounded in Bayes' theorem. The Naïve Bayes algorithm assumes independence between features, which simplifies the computation process. Variants like Multinomial Naïve Bayes and Bernoulli Naïve Bayes have shown particularly impressive performance in sentiment analysis tasks, especially when BoW or TF-IDF representations are employed. Despite its simplicity, Naïve Bayes performs well for sentiment analysis, making it a reliable choice in many cases.

Support Vector Machines (SVM) represent a more sophisticated approach to sentiment classification. SVM works by finding the best hyperplane that separates different sentiment classes in a high-dimensional feature space. SVM is highly regarded for its robustness and ability to handle complex and high-dimensional data. When paired with well-engineered text features, it can be particularly powerful in distinguishing between different sentiment classes, making it a strong candidate for many sentiment classification tasks.

Finally, Random Forest, an ensemble learning method, combines the predictions of multiple decision trees to improve classification accuracy. While less commonly used than other models in sentiment analysis, Random Forest can be effective, particularly in cases where the data is noisy or inconsistent. Its ability to aggregate results from several trees allows it to capture various aspects of the data, making it robust in handling diverse inputs.

Deep Learning-Based Sentiment Analysis

Deep learning has significantly improved sentiment analysis accuracy by enabling models to learn complex contextual relationships in text. Unlike traditional ML models, deep learning models do not require extensive manual feature engineering. Instead, they use large neural networks and pre-trained word embeddings to capture semantic meaning.

Word Embeddings with Deep Learning

Traditional text representations like BoW and TF-IDF ignore word meanings and relationships. Word embeddings, such as Word2Vec and GloVe, solve this problem by representing words as dense numerical vectors, capturing their semantic relationships. These embeddings serve as input features for deep learning models.

RNN and LSTM Models

Since text data has sequential dependencies, Recurrent Neural Networks (RNNs) and Long Short-Term Memory (LSTM) models are widely used for sentiment analysis. LSTMs improve upon standard RNNs by addressing the issue of long-term dependencies, making them suitable for analyzing longer text sequences.

Transformer-Based Models

Modern NLP models use transformer-based architectures, such as BERT (Bidirectional Encoder Representations from Transformers), RoBERTa, and DistilBERT, which achieve state-of-the-art sentiment classification accuracy. These models use bidirectional context understanding, making them highly effective for complex sentiment analysis tasks.

Steps to Train a Sentiment Classifier

To build an effective sentiment classifier using machine learning, the following steps are typically followed:

1. Data Preprocessing

Before training a sentiment classifier, text data must be preprocessed. This involves:

- Removing punctuation, special characters, and stopwords

- Lowercasing text to standardize format.

- Tokenization (splitting text into words or subwords)

- Lemmatization or stemming to reduce words to their root forms.

2. Feature Extraction

Once the text is cleaned, it needs to be converted into numerical representations using these:

- Bag of Words (BoW): Represents text as a frequency-based word matrix.

- TF-IDF (Term Frequency-Inverse Document Frequency): Weighs words based on importance in a document.

- Word Embeddings (Word2Vec, GloVe, FastText): Captures word relationships and semantics in dense vectors.

3. Model Training and Evaluation

After feature extraction, the sentiment classifier is trained using a machine learning or deep learning model. The model is evaluated using metrics such as accuracy, precision, recall, and F1-score to measure its performance.

Example

A small online clothing retailer wants to better understand how customers feel about their products. They collect hundreds of customer reviews from their website, with comments like "Love the fabric and fit!" or "The stitching came apart after one wash." The team uses a machine learning approach to automate the process of sorting these reviews as positive, negative, or neutral. First, they clean and prepare the text, removing extra characters and standardizing the format. Then they use labeled past reviews—ones they already know are positive or negative—to train a logistic regression model. The model learns patterns in the language, such as words like "love," "comfortable," and "disappointed." After training, the model is used to analyze new reviews as they come in, flagging negative ones for follow-up and identifying common praise for marketing use. Over time, as the model is fed more examples, its accuracy improves. The retailer now saves hours of manual review and can respond more quickly to customer concerns.

Review Questions

1. What's the difference between machine learning and rule-based sentiment analysis?
2. Name two machine learning models for sentiment analysis.
3. What are word embeddings and why are they important?
4. Why are RNNs and LSTMs good for sentiment analysis?
5. How does BERT improve sentiment analysis?
6. What steps are needed to build a sentiment analysis model?
7. How is TF-IDF different from Bag of Words?
8. What metrics evaluate a sentiment model?
9. When is Random Forest preferred for sentiment analysis?
10. What's the difference between traditional ML and deep learning for sentiment analysis?

4-4 Sentiment Analysis Applications

Learning Outcomes

4-4-1 Describe how sentiment analysis is used in different industries.

4-4-2 Explain how businesses use social media sentiment to track public opinion.

4-4-3 Understand how reviews (e.g., Amazon, IMDb) are analyzed for product and movie feedback.

4-4-4 Identify how companies use customer sentiment to improve services and support.

4-4-5 Recognize how sentiment analysis helps in financial forecasting and trading.

Sentiment analysis has become a powerful tool in various industries, enabling businesses, organizations, and researchers to gain insights into public opinion, customer feedback, and market trends. By analyzing text data from social media, product reviews, customer interactions, and financial news, sentiment analysis helps in decision-making, trend forecasting, and improving services. This section explores key applications of sentiment analysis across different domains.

Use Cases of Sentiment Analysis

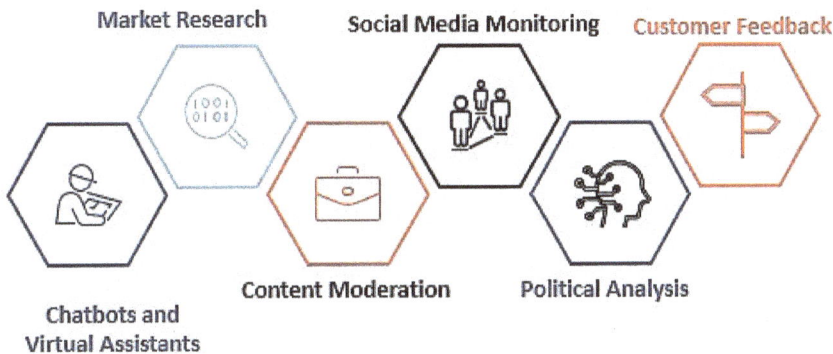

Market Research   Social Media Monitoring   Customer Feedback

Content Moderation   Political Analysis

Chatbots and Virtual Assistants

Social Media Analysis

Tracking Public Opinion

Social media platforms like Twitter, Facebook, and Reddit generate massive amounts of user-generated content daily. Sentiment analysis helps in tracking public opinion on several topics, including current events, social issues, and emerging trends. Companies, governments, and researchers use sentiment analysis to check discussions and understand how people feel about topics.

For example, during a major event like the Olympics or a political election, sentiment analysis can track how opinions evolve over time. By analyzing hashtags, comments, and discussions, organizations can measure public sentiment and respond accordingly.

Trends for Brands and Political Campaigns

Brands use sentiment analysis to gauge customer feeling and brand reputation. By analyzing social media mentions and reviews, companies can detect whether their products and services are viewed positively or negatively. For example, a company launching a new product can watch real-time reactions to assess customer satisfaction and address concerns.

Similarly, political campaigns use sentiment analysis to measure voter sentiment. Politicians and campaign teams analyze public discourse on social media to identify key issues, shape messaging strategies, and predict election outcomes.

Product and Movie Reviews

Analyzing Reviews

Online reviews play a crucial role in consumer decision-making. Sentiment analysis of reviews from platforms like Amazon, Yelp, and IMDb allows businesses to understand customer satisfaction and areas for improvement. For instance, analyzing customer reviews on Amazon helps companies find common complaints about a product, such as poor battery life or durability issues.

For movie studios, sentiment analysis of IMDb and Rotten Tomatoes reviews provide insights into audience reactions. If a film receives negative sentiment before its official release, marketing strategies can be adjusted to address concerns or improve promotional efforts.

Predicting Based on Customer Feedback

Sentiment analysis can also be used to predict the success of a product by analyzing early reviews. A product receiving overwhelmingly positive feedback is more likely to succeed in the market. Similarly, businesses can use sentiment trends to refine their offerings, such as changing product features based on customer feedback before a wider release.

Customer Feedback Analysis

Improving Business Strategies

Understanding customer sentiment is essential for businesses looking to enhance their products, services, and overall customer experience. Sentiment analysis allows companies to find patterns in customer feedback and make data-driven improvements. For example, an airline company may analyze customer feedback from surveys and social media posts to figure out if passengers are dissatisfied with flight delays or customer service, leading to operational adjustments.

Automated Sentiment Monitoring

Customer service departments are increasingly using sentiment analysis in automated chatbots to improve interactions. Chatbots equipped with sentiment analysis capabilities can detect customer emotions in real time and adjust responses accordingly. For instance, if a chatbot detects frustration in a customer's messages, it can escalate the issue to a human agent or offer personalized solutions. This enhances customer satisfaction and helps businesses provide more efficient service.

Financial and Stock Market Predictions

Predict Market Trends

In the financial sector, sentiment analysis is used to analyze news articles, financial reports, and social media discussions to predict stock market trends. Investors and analysts examine the sentiment of financial news and social media conversations to assess market sentiment. If sentiment analysis shows a surge in positive discussions about a particular company, it may signal potential stock price growth.

For example, during a product launch or major company announcement, sentiment analysis of public reactions can provide early indicators of how the stock market will respond. This helps traders make informed investment decisions.

Sentiment-Based Trading Algorithms

Sentiment-based trading algorithms use real-time sentiment data to execute trades automatically. These algorithms analyze news headlines, earnings reports, and financial tweets to find trading opportunities. If a sudden spike in negative sentiment is detected for a company, the algorithm may sell stocks before their value drops. Conversely, if a stock receives positive sentiment from influential financial analysts, the algorithm may start a buy order.

Hedge funds and financial institutions integrate sentiment analysis into their trading strategies to gain a competitive edge in fast-moving markets. By combining sentiment data with traditional financial indicators, these algorithms enhance decision-making and improve portfolio performance.

Review Questions

1. How is sentiment analysis used to track public opinion on social media?
2. Why do brands use sentiment analysis after launching a product?
3. How can sentiment analysis of reviews help predict a product's success?
4. Give an example of how a business might use sentiment data to improve customer service.
5. What role does sentiment analysis play in chatbots?
6. How can financial analysts use sentiment analysis to predict stock trends?
7. What are sentiment-based trading algorithms?
8. Why is customer feedback important for business strategy?
9. How do political campaigns benefit from sentiment analysis?
10. What kinds of text data are commonly analyzed for sentiment in finance?

Chapter 5

Named Entity Recognition (NER)

5-1 What is NER?

Definition

Named Entity Recognition (NER) is a core task in Natural Language Processing (NLP) that involves identifying and classifying named entities in text into predefined categories such as people, organizations, locations, dates, monetary values, percentages, and more. NER systems analyze unstructured text data and extract these entities, making them structured and more accessible for downstream processes like data analysis, machine learning, and information retrieval.

Importance of NER in NLP

NER is of paramount importance in NLP because it serves as a foundational tool for understanding and processing natural language. In a world where vast amounts of unstructured text data exist, whether in documents, social media posts, or emails, NER helps to sift through this data and find the key components that carry significant meaning. By extracting specific entities from text, NER allows machines to understand which aspects of the content are most relevant, such as the names of people, organizations, or places. This structured information is then used to perform more complex tasks like question answering, automatic summarization, and sentiment analysis.

Moreover, NER enhances the ability to automate and scale the processing of copious amounts of text data. For example, in content extraction or data mining, NER helps find and categorize information, thus enabling efficient data processing and retrieval. Without NER, extracting actionable insights from raw text would be far more difficult and time-consuming, making this task a critical part of any NLP-based application.

How NER Helps Extract Information

Unstructured text, which lacks a predefined structure, is common in natural language. NER helps transform this unorganized data into structured information by finding and tagging named entities. These entities are then categorized into specific groups, such as persons (e.g., "Albert Einstein"), organizations (e.g., "Microsoft"), locations (e.g., "Paris") or dates and times (e.g., "January 1, 2025").

By doing this, NER extracts valuable information from raw text and organizes it in a manner that is easier for computers to analyze. The structured output from NER can be used to populate databases, improve search engines, or provide insights for applications such as chatbots and recommendation systems. This process allows businesses and researchers to automate tasks that would otherwise require manual data entry or sifting through vast quantities of text.

Overview of How NER Works

NER is applied in a variety of contexts, all of which receive help from the extraction of structured data from unstructured text. For example, in information retrieval systems, NER helps improve search accuracy by recognizing key terms such as the names of companies, people, or locations. In social media analysis, NER can be used to find trends, track mentions of brands or individuals and analyze sentiments toward specific entities.

NER is also heavily used in fields such as healthcare and finance. In healthcare, it can be used to extract relevant medical terms, drug names, and patient information from clinical records. In finance, NER aids in finding market trends, company mentions, and financial terms within financial news articles, reports, and filings. By transforming unstructured text into structured data, NER opens a range of possibilities for automating the extraction and analysis of key information.

Challenges in Entity Recognition

Ambiguous Entities

One of the most significant challenges in NER is handling ambiguous entities. For instance, the word "Apple" can refer to the technology company, the fruit, or even a music label. Differentiating between these meanings depends heavily on context, and this can be an arduous task for NER systems to perform accurately. Resolving ambiguity is particularly challenging when the context is limited or unclear, and errors can lead to misclassifications that affect the quality of downstream processes.

Contextual Variations in Entity Mentions

Entities can be mentioned in many different forms, making them difficult to recognize consistently. For example, a company may be referred to by its full name, an abbreviation, or even a nickname. "International Business Machines" may be shortened to "IBM," and "United States" may be referred to as "USA" or simply "America." These variations require NER systems to be flexible and capable of recognizing different representations of the same entity. Not accounting for such variations can lead to incomplete or inaccurate entity recognition.

Handling Misspellings and Abbreviations

Another challenge in NER is handling misspellings and abbreviations. Text data, particularly in informal settings like social media, often has typos, slang, and non-standard abbreviations that can confuse NER models. For example, "Google" might be misspelled as "Googlr" or abbreviated in a hashtag such as "#Goog." Such variations can hinder the ability of NER systems to find the intended entity, leading to errors in entity extraction and classification.

1. What is Named Entity Recognition (NER)?
2. Why is NER important in Natural Language Processing?
3. What are some examples of entities NER can identify?
4. What makes recognizing the word "Apple" a challenge for NER?
5. How do name variations (like "IBM" vs. "International Business Machines") affect NER?
6. Why is handling misspellings and abbreviations difficult for NER systems?

5-2 Types of Named Entities

Learning Outcomes

5-2-1 List common types of named entities (e.g., people, places, organizations).

5-2-2 Explain why these entities matter in text analysis.

5-2-3 Recognize domain-specific entities in fields like medicine, law, and finance.

5-2-4 Understand the purpose of custom NER models.

Named Entity Recognition (NER) is a process that names and categorizes key pieces of information in unstructured text, known as named entities. These entities can be classified into several types, ranging from general categories such as people, organizations, and locations to more domain-specific entities in fields like healthcare, law, and finance. Understanding the distinct types of named entities is crucial for accurately interpreting and organizing text data for different applications.

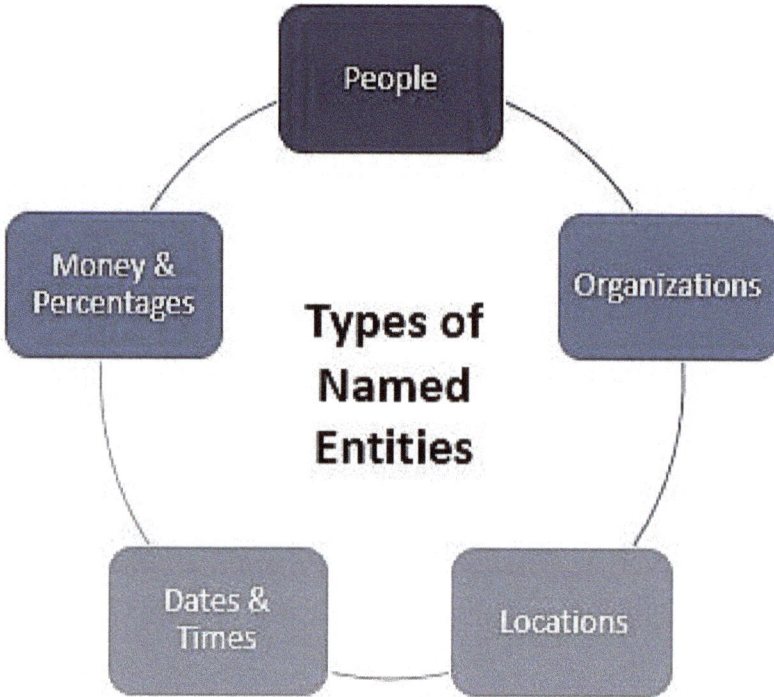

Standard Named Entities

The most common types of named entities found in NER are standard categories that apply broadly across various texts and domains. These include:

People

People are one of the most recognizable types of named entities. This category includes names of individuals, such as "Elon Musk" or "Barack Obama." Finding the names of people is critical in a variety of applications, from news analysis to social media sentiment analysis. Recognizing the names of public figures helps machines understand the text and relate it to the proper person or entity.

Organizations

Organizations, which can refer to businesses, institutions, government agencies, or other formal entities, are another standard category of named entities. Examples include "Google," "United Nations," or "World Health Organization." Recognizing organizations is vital for tasks such as news aggregation, business intelligence, and automated research, where understanding the role of an organization in a text can provide essential context.

Locations

Locations, including geographic locations such as cities, countries, mountains, rivers, and landmarks, are also commonly recognized by NER systems. Examples include "New York," "Mount Everest," or "Amazon River." Recognizing locations is essential for geographic information systems (GIS), travel-related applications, and understanding the spatial context of events or news stories.

Date and Time Expressions

Dates and time expressions are critical for contextualizing events in a timeline. Examples include specific dates like "January 1, 2023," or time expressions such as "2:30 PM." Recognizing these entities allows systems to organize events chronologically, which is useful in news articles, historical data analysis, and scheduling applications.

Monetary Values

Monetary values, including both amounts and currencies, are another important category. Examples include "$100," "€50 million," or "¥500." Extracting monetary values helps in various fields such as financial news analysis, economic reports, and e-commerce, where precise understanding of financial data is essential for making informed decisions.

Percentages

Percentages such as "45% growth" or "10% reduction" are also categorized as named entities in NER. Percentages are often used to describe financial changes, market trends, or statistical data. Recognizing percentages helps systems to track performance metrics and quantify changes in fields like economics, marketing, and business analysis.

Domain-Specific Named Entities

In addition to the standard types of named entities, NER can also be tailored to specific domains where unique entities require recognition. These domain-specific entities are crucial for more specialized applications:

Medical Entities

In the healthcare and medical fields, NER systems are trained to find specific entities such as diseases, drug names, medical procedures, and treatments. For instance, entities like "Alzheimer's disease," "Aspirin," or "chemotherapy" are commonly found in medical texts. Recognizing these entities helps medical professionals and researchers efficiently process clinical records, research papers, and patient data to make informed decisions about healthcare.

Legal Entities

In legal contexts, NER systems focus on extracting information from case laws, statutes, regulations, and contracts. Legal entities can include specific case names like "Brown v. Board of Education," legal terms such as "habeas corpus," or references to laws and acts like "The Civil Rights Act." Accurate recognition of legal entities is essential in legal research, contract analysis, and automated legal services.

Financial Entities

Financial entities include terms relevant to the economic and financial sectors, such as stock market symbols, economic indicators, and market reports. For example, "AAPL" (Apple's stock symbol), "NASDAQ," or "GDP growth rate" are financial entities. Recognizing financial entities allows financial analysts, investors, and news outlets to track market performance, analyze trends, and provide insights into economic conditions.

Custom Named Entity Recognition

While many NER systems are designed to recognize standard and domain-specific named entities, there is also the possibility of customizing NER models to suit the needs of industries or applications. This process involves training NER models on industry-specific datasets that may have specialized terminology or named entities not covered by standard or pre-existing models.

For example, in the field of pharmaceuticals, a custom NER model may be trained to find specific drug names, clinical trials, or pharmaceutical companies. Similarly, in the technology sector, a customized model may focus on finding software products, coding languages, or tech startups. Custom NER models enable companies to extract valuable insights from industry-specific documents, reports, and datasets, enhancing their ability to process and analyze textual data that is unique to their sector.

Review Questions

1. What are the main types of named entities in NER?
2. Why is it useful to recognize names of people and organizations?
3. How do location and date entities help interpret text?
4. What are domain-specific entities? Give one example.
5. Why would someone create a custom NER model?

5-3 Rule vs. Machine Learning-Based NER

Learning Outcomes

5-3-1 Distinguish between rule-based and machine learning–based NER systems.

5-3-2 Describe how rule-based systems use dictionaries, patterns, and regex.

5-3-3 Explain traditional machine learning approaches like CRFs and HMMs.

5-3-4 Summarize the role of deep learning (e.g., LSTM, BERT) in modern NER.

5-3-5 Compare the strengths and weaknesses of both approaches.

Named Entity Recognition (NER) is a critical task in Natural Language Processing (NLP) that enables machines to name and classify entities such as people, organizations, locations, dates, and other significant terms in text. There are two primary approaches to NER: rule-based and machine learning-based. Each approach has its strengths and weaknesses, and the choice between the two depends on the specific application, dataset, and computational resources available.

Rule-Based NER

Rule-based NER systems rely on predefined rules, lexicons, and patterns to find entities in text. These systems use a combination of dictionaries, regular expressions, and handcrafted rules to find and classify named entities.

Lexicons, Dictionaries, and Patterns

A rule-based NER system typically uses a set of predefined lexicons and dictionaries that have a list of known entities, such as names of people, organizations, and locations. When a word or phrase in the text matches an entry in one of these dictionaries, the system can tag it as a named entity. Additionally, patterns and syntactic rules are applied to help find entities in context. For example, a pattern might specify that a capitalized word following a title (such as "Mr." or "Dr.") is likely to be a person's name.

Regular Expressions for Entity Extraction

Regular expressions (regex) are often used in rule-based NER systems to find patterns in text. A regex pattern could match specific formats, such as dates (e.g., "MM/DD/YYYY") or monetary values (e.g., "$100" or "€50 million"). These patterns are particularly useful for extracting specific types of entities that follow a predictable structure. Regular expressions allow for a high degree of precision in an entity extraction if the entity follows the defined pattern.

Strengths of Rule-Based NER

One of the primary advantages of rule-based NER is its speed. Since the system uses predefined rules and dictionaries, it can quickly process text and find named entities. Additionally, rule-based systems are highly interpretable. Users can directly view and change the rules, which makes it easier to understand how the system makes its decisions. This interpretability is valuable when debugging or refining the system. Rule-based systems are also effective when working with structured or well-formed text, where entities tend to follow specific patterns and conventions.

Weaknesses of Rule-Based NER

Despite these strengths, rule-based NER systems have several limitations. One of the most significant drawbacks is their limited adaptability. These systems rely on predefined rules, so they are not easily able to adapt to new or unseen entities. This makes them less suitable for tasks that require generalization across diverse datasets or contexts. Rule-based systems are also difficult to scale, especially when working with large, diverse, or noisy datasets. As the variety of entities increases, the rule set must be constantly updated and refined, which can become a time-consuming and cumbersome process. Additionally, rule-based systems struggle with handling ambiguity, as they cannot easily resolve conflicting meanings in context.

Example

Imagine a company developing a rule-based NER system to extract named entities from a large collection of financial news articles. The developers begin by compiling a set of lexicons, including lists of well-known banks, corporations, countries, and job titles. When the system encounters the sentence, "On April 15, 2024, CEO Angela Martinez of GreenWave Holdings announced a 50 million investment in renewable energy," it uses these dictionaries and handcrafted rules to identify and label entities. The date "April 15, 2024" matches a regular expression pattern for standard date formats, so it is tagged as a DATE entity. The capitalized word "CEO" followed by a capitalized full name matches a pattern indicating a PERSON entity, so "Angela Martinez" is tagged accordingly. The phrase "GreenWave Holdings" appears in the organization lexicon and is labeled as an ORGANIZATION. Lastly, the monetary amount "50 million" fits a regex for currency values, allowing it to be extracted as a MONEY entity. By combining dictionaries, syntactic rules (like titles before names), and regular expressions for patterns, the system can accurately identify structured entities in the text. However, if a new company name or a colloquial reference to an entity appears that isn't in the lexicon or doesn't follow a known pattern, the system may fail to recognize it—highlighting both the strengths and limits of rule-based approaches.

Rule-Based vs. ML-Based NER

Feature	Rule-Based NER	ML-Based NER
Approach	Uses dictionaries & rules	Learns from labeled data
Techniques	Applies patterns & regex	CRF, HMM, LSTM, BERT
Performance	Fast and interpretable	Handles context and ambiguity
Best For	Structured or predictable text	Complex, varied, or ambiguous language
Adaptability	Limited, needs constant updates	Improves with more data
Training Need	No training needed	Requires large labeled datasets
Computational Cost	Low	High

Machine Learning-Based NER

Machine learning-based NER approaches use statistical models and algorithms to automatically learn patterns and relationships in text data. These systems can improve over time as they are exposed to more data and are capable of recognizing entities in a broader range of contexts.

Traditional Machine Learning Approaches

Earlier machine learning-based Named Entity Recognition (NER) systems relied on traditional machine learning models such as Conditional Random Fields (CRF) and Hidden Markov Models (HMM). Conditional Random Fields (CRF) are probabilistic graphical models primarily used for sequence labeling tasks like NER. CRFs model the relationship between input features—such as words and part-of-speech tags—and output labels, which in the case of NER, would be entity types like person, location, or organization. One of the key advantages of CRFs is their ability to capture dependencies between adjacent labels, allowing the model to consider the context in which entities appear. This sequential nature of CRFs helps improve the accuracy of entity recognition, making them a popular choice for NER tasks.

On the other hand, Hidden Markov Models (HMM) are statistical models that predict a sequence of hidden states based on observed data. In NER, HMMs are used to label each word in a sentence with a corresponding entity type. HMMs excel in structured text where entities follow known patterns, making them suitable for tasks where the relationships between words are predictable. However, they can struggle when dealing with unstructured or noisy data. Despite this limitation, HMMs have been widely used in the past for named entity recognition, particularly when the textual data exhibits regularity and structure.

Both CRFs and HMMs have been foundational in traditional machine learning approaches to NER, with each method offering distinct advantages depending on the nature of the data and the task at hand. However, more recent advancements in deep learning techniques have begun to outperform these traditional methods in handling more complex and varied types of text data.

Example

Consider a team building a machine learning–based NER system to extract entities from medical reports. Rather than relying on predefined rules, they use a labeled dataset where each word in the text is annotated with its corresponding entity type, such as "PatientName," "Disease," or "Medication." They train a Conditional Random Field (CRF) model using features like the word itself, its part-of-speech tag, capitalization, and neighboring words. When the model processes a sentence like "Patient Jane Doe was diagnosed with Type 2 diabetes and prescribed Metformin," it learns from context that "Jane Doe" is a person's name (a typical noun phrase following "Patient"), "Type 2 diabetes" is a disease (often following "diagnosed with"), and "Metformin" is a medication (commonly found after "prescribed"). The CRF captures these dependencies and accurately assigns entity labels. In another scenario, the team might use a Hidden Markov Model (HMM) to label sequences in highly structured discharge summaries. The HMM predicts the most likely sequence of entity tags based on word transitions and prior probabilities, performing well in environments where the format of reports is consistent. Both models adapt to patterns in the data rather than relying on hardcoded rules, allowing them to generalize beyond the training examples—though their performance still depends heavily on the quality and representativeness of the training data.

Deep Learning-Based Approaches

More recently, deep learning-based approaches have revolutionized Named Entity Recognition (NER), offering higher accuracy and the ability to learn complex patterns from large datasets. One of the key models in this area is Recurrent Neural Networks (RNNs), particularly when paired with Long Short-Term Memory (LSTM) networks. RNNs are designed to handle sequential data, making them highly effective for tasks such as NER, where the order of words and the context within a sentence are important. LSTMs, a specific type of RNN, are particularly useful because they can capture long-range dependencies in text. This capability is crucial for understanding the context of named entities, especially over longer spans of text. By considering both the current word and the surrounding context, LSTMs can learn to recognize entities more accurately, even in complex sentences.

In addition to RNNs and LSTMs, Transformer-based models have also become central to modern NER systems. Transformer models, particularly BERT (Bidirectional Encoder Representations from Transformers), have achieved state-of-the-art performance across a variety of natural language processing tasks, including NER. Unlike RNNs, which process text sequentially, Transformer models process the entire input text at once, allowing them to understand the contextual meaning of words by considering their relationships with all other words in the sentence simultaneously. This bidirectional approach enables models like BERT to capture complex relationships between words and entities, significantly improving the accuracy of entity recognition. Furthermore, tools like spaCy and Flair have integrated Transformer models to provide robust and highly accurate NER solutions, making deep learning the dominant approach in modern NER systems.

> **Example**
>
> A healthcare analytics company is developing a deep learning–based NER system to extract critical medical entities from unstructured clinical notes. Instead of using predefined rules or traditional models, they train a Bidirectional LSTM (BiLSTM) model on a large corpus of annotated medical texts. When processing the sentence, "The patient was referred to Dr. Emily Chen at Stanford Medical Center for evaluation of chronic kidney disease," the BiLSTM uses both the left and right context of each word to determine its role. This bidirectional context allows the model to correctly identify "Dr. Emily Chen" as a PERSON entity, "Stanford Medical Center" as an ORGANIZATION, and "chronic kidney disease" as a DISEASE, even though these phrases vary in length and position. To further boost performance, the team fine-tunes a BERT-based model on the same dataset. Unlike RNNs, BERT processes the entire sentence at once and captures intricate relationships between words using self-attention mechanisms. This enables it to distinguish between "Apple" as a company and "apple" as a fruit, based solely on context. When applied to thousands of clinical notes, the BERT-based NER system consistently outperforms earlier models, offering high precision in identifying complex and domain-specific entities. The team integrates the model into an NLP pipeline using spaCy, enabling accurate real-time extraction of medical terms from patient records—demonstrating the power and flexibility of deep learning approaches in modern NER tasks.

Strengths of Machine Learning-Based NER

The strengths of machine learning-based NER are particularly clear in their high accuracy and ability to learn from context. These systems can recognize named entities even in noisy or unstructured text, and they improve over time as they are exposed to more data. Unlike rule-based systems, machine learning-based models can handle ambiguities and contextual variations, making them more adaptable and scalable. They can also generalize across diverse datasets, recognizing entities in a wide range of contexts and domains.

Weaknesses of Machine Learning-Based NER

However, machine learning-based NER comes with its own set of challenges. One of the primary drawbacks is the need for large, labeled datasets. To train a high-performing model, a substantial amount of annotated data is needed, which can be expensive and time-consuming to gather. Additionally, machine learning-based models, particularly deep learning models, are computationally expensive and require significant resources to train. This can be a barrier for organizations with limited access to powerful hardware or cloud-based services.

Review Questions

1. What are the main features of rule-based NER systems?
2. How are regular expressions used in rule-based NER?
3. What are CRFs and how do they support NER?
4. How do deep learning models like BERT improve NER performance?
5. What are key advantages and limitations of machine learning–based NER?

5-4 Real-World Use Cases

Learning Outcomes

5-4-1 Define Named Entity Recognition (NER) and its purpose.

5-4-2 Describe how NER improves chatbots and virtual assistants.

5-4-3 Identify uses of NER in document analysis (law, medicine, finance).

5-4-4 Explain how NER helps in monitoring news and social media.

5-4-5 Summarize how e-commerce uses NER for customer insights.

5-4-6 Recognize the role of NER in healthcare and research.

Named Entity Recognition (NER) plays a significant role in various real-world applications, allowing for the extraction and categorization of meaningful entities from unstructured text. By naming key terms such as names, locations, dates, and other domain-specific entities, NER enables systems to make sense of complex data and automate processes.

Chatbots and Virtual Assistants

Chatbots and virtual assistants have become integral components of customer service, offering automated responses and help in various industries. NER plays a crucial role in enhancing the performance of these systems by extracting key entities such as names, locations, and dates, which can be used to tailor interactions and provide personalized responses.

For example, when a user interacts with a virtual assistant to schedule an appointment, NER can help find the date, time, and location mentioned in the conversation. By recognizing entities like "Monday," "10:00 AM," and "New York," the system can offer a more contextually proper response, such as confirming the appointment or suggesting available time slots. Similarly, in customer support, NER helps extract relevant details from a user's inquiry, such as order numbers or product names, to provide correct and personalized help.

Furthermore, chatbots and virtual assistants rely on NER to understand and respond to user queries efficiently. By recognizing the entities mentioned in the text, these systems can give precise answers, making user interactions more seamless and satisfying. This enhances the overall customer experience and reduces the need for human intervention, particularly in high-volume customer support scenarios.

Information Extraction from Documents

NER is particularly useful in automating the extraction of critical information from various types of documents, especially in fields like law, medicine, and finance. These industries rely on vast amounts of textual data, and NER helps to distill relevant entities from these documents, saving time and effort in manual data extraction.

In the legal industry, NER systems can find key legal entities such as case names, statutes, and legal terms within contracts and case law. This can streamline legal research, enabling lawyers and paralegals to quickly find important sections of legal documents without having to read entire files. In the medical field, NER is used to extract mentions of diseases, drug names, and treatment plans from clinical records, medical research papers, or patient data. This aids healthcare professionals quickly finding critical medical information, improving decision-making and patient care.

Moreover, in the financial sector, NER can automatically extract relevant financial figures, company names, and economic indicators from annual reports, financial statements, and market analyses. By automating the extraction of such entities, businesses can quickly summarize and analyze large volumes of financial data, helping better strategic planning and decision-making.

News and Social Media Monitoring

NER is widely used in news and social media monitoring to track trending topics, find key players, and detect emerging events. Media outlets, public relations firms, and marketing teams rely on NER to watch vast amounts of content from news articles, blogs, and social media platforms. By extracting named entities such as the names of public figures, organizations, locations, and events, these systems can automatically detect the most relevant and widely discussed topics.

For example, NER can name the names of politicians, celebrities, or businesses in news articles, helping analysts track the public discourse surrounding these entities. This is particularly useful for businesses, watching their brand reputation or for government agencies tracking discussions around policy issues. Additionally, NER helps in the detection of misinformation and fake news by showing false claims, inconsistencies, and misattributions of information. By extracting key entities and cross-referencing them with reliable sources, NER systems can help name potential misinformation and flag it for further review.

Social media platforms also receive help from NER in identifying user discussions around trending topics, events, or product launches. This allows organizations to analyze user sentiment, track brand mentions, and engage with audiences more effectively. By detecting key entities in real-time, businesses can stay ahead of market trends and capitalize on emerging opportunities.

E-Commerce and Customer Insights

In e-commerce, NER is increasingly being used to extract valuable insights from customer reviews, social media posts, and other user-generated content. By recognizing entities such as product names, brands, and features, NER helps companies analyze customer feedback more efficiently and understand consumer preferences.

For example, NER can extract mentions of specific products or brands in customer reviews, allowing businesses to show which products are receiving the most attention and which features customers value the most. This can help in improving product offerings, targeting advertising campaigns, or addressing customer concerns in a timely manner. NER is also used to analyze discussions around new product launches or promotions on social media, enabling businesses to gauge public opinion and make data-driven decisions.

Additionally, NER is valuable in sentiment analysis, where it helps find entities linked to positive or negative sentiments. For instance, by extracting product names or brand mentions alongside sentiment markers (e.g., "love," "hate"), businesses can gain insights into how customers feel about specific products, which can inform product development and marketing strategies.

Healthcare and Biomedical Research

The healthcare and biomedical research sectors rely heavily on correct information extraction to advance medical knowledge and improve patient care. NER plays a pivotal role in finding relevant medical terms, such as drug names, diseases, symptoms, and medical conditions, from research papers, clinical records, and medical literature.

In biomedical research, NER is used to extract entities from scientific articles, including mentions of specific diseases, medications, clinical trials, and research findings. This allows researchers to quickly access relevant information and stay updated on the latest developments in their field. By automating this process, NER helps researchers focus on more complex tasks such as hypothesis generation and experimental design, rather than manual data extraction.

NER is also instrumental in electronic health record (EHR) analysis, where it can find critical medical entities such as patient conditions, treatments, and test results. This enables healthcare providers to quickly access patient histories and make informed decisions about diagnoses and treatment plans. By extracting relevant entities from EHRs, NER helps streamline the workflow of healthcare professionals, improving patient outcomes.

Review Questions

1. What does NER do?
2. How does NER help chatbots?
3. Name one use of NER in document analysis.
4. How is NER used in social media monitoring?
5. How can NER help e-commerce businesses?
6. What is one way NER supports healthcare?
7. How does NER help with sentiment analysis?
8. How can NER help detect fake news?

Chapter 6

Topic Modeling

6-1 Introduction to Topic Modeling

Learning Outcomes

6-1-1 Define topic modeling and explain its purpose.

6-1-2 Distinguish between topic modeling and text classification.

6-1-3 Describe why topic modeling is important in NLP.

6-1-4 Identify common use cases of topic modeling in real-world applications.

6-1-5 Name key unsupervised techniques used for topic modeling (e.g., LDA, NMF, LSA).

Topic modeling is an essential technique in Natural Language Processing (NLP) that allows machines to automatically discover the underlying themes or topics within a collection of documents. This powerful tool enables organizations and researchers to analyze large volumes of unstructured text, helping them uncover patterns, insights, and trends that would be difficult or time-consuming to find manually.

What is Topic Modeling?

Topic modeling is an unsupervised machine learning technique used to analyze large collections of text and extract latent or hidden topics that are
represented as clusters of words. These topics are inferred from the co-
occurrence patterns of words across documents. The goal of topic modeling is to find groups of words that often appear together in the same context
and then associate these word groups with specific topics. Each document
in the dataset is then represented as a mixture of those topics, with different
proportions of each topic in every document.

What Topic Modeling Does

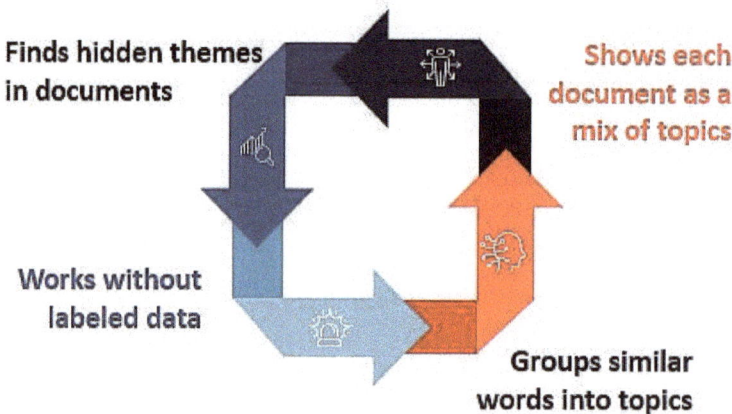

Finds hidden themes in documents

Shows each document as a mix of topics

Works without labeled data

Groups similar words into topics

Importance in NLP

Topic modeling plays a crucial role in Natural Language Processing because
it helps convert unstructured textual data into structured, interpretable insights. With the increasing availability of vast amounts of unstructured text—

such as news articles, academic papers, social media posts, and customer reviews—topic modeling allows organizations to process and analyze this information at scale.

The importance of topic modeling lies in its ability to extract high-level themes from large datasets without the need for labeled data, making it highly useful for exploratory analysis. It can help reveal trends, patterns, and relationships within a body of text, offering valuable insights that might not be at once obvious. For example, businesses can use topic modeling to understand customer feedback, find emerging trends, and watch sentiment. In academic research, topic modeling can help scholars uncover underlying themes in a large corpus of papers, enabling a more comprehensive understanding of a field.

Moreover, topic modeling can be used to reduce the dimensionality of textual data, making it easier to analyze. By summarizing a large corpus with a small set of topics, it allows for more efficient search, retrieval, and categorization of documents, which is particularly useful in information retrieval systems.

Compare to Text Classification

Topic Modeling vs. Text Classification

Feature	Topic Modeling	Text Classification
Type	Unsupervised	Supervised
Labels	Not needed	Required
Output	Topics per document	One label per document
Use Case	Explore themes	Categorize known classes

Although both topic modeling and text classification are important techniques in NLP, they serve different purposes and work differently. Text classification is a supervised learning task, where the goal is to assign a predefined label to a given document based on its content. For example, a text classification model might categorize emails as "spam" or "not spam" or assign news articles to topics such as "sports," "politics," or "entertainment." The model is trained on a labeled dataset, where each document is already associated with a specific label.

In contrast, topic modeling is an unsupervised learning technique, meaning it does not require labeled data. Instead, it shows underlying patterns in the text itself to extract topics. The topics are not predefined, and the goal is not to assign a specific label to each document, but to uncover the hidden themes within a corpus. Unlike text classification, where the labels are decided by human annotators, topic modeling allows the data itself to reveal the structure of the text.

Another key difference is that text classification typically focuses on assigning a single label or category to a document, while topic modeling can produce multiple topics for each document, reflecting the complexity and diversity of the content. A document can be about multiple topics simultaneously, while in text classification, each document is usually assigned to a single, most relevant category.

Use Cases for Topic Modeling

Topic modeling has a wide range of applications across various industries and fields. Some of the most common use cases include:

Customer Feedback Analysis

Businesses can use topic modeling to analyze customer reviews, support tickets, or social media mentions to understand common themes, find product issues, and uncover emerging trends. For instance, by applying topic modeling to customer feedback, a company could find that many customers are discussing "shipping delays" or "product quality," allowing the company to act accordingly.

Content Recommendation

Topic modeling is widely used in content-based recommendation systems. By analyzing the topics of documents or articles, a system can recommend updated content that aligns with the topics of interest to the user. For example, a news website might recommend articles on related topics (e.g., "technology," "politics") based on a user's reading history.

Social Media Monitoring: Topic modeling can be used to track and analyze discussions on social media platforms. By naming the main topics being discussed, businesses, governments, or organizations can monitor public sentiment, track trends, and engage in real-time conversations on relevant topics.

Academic Research and Literature Review

Researchers can use topic modeling to analyze a large corpus of academic papers and show the main themes within a specific research area. This can help scholars quickly understand the key topics being discussed in a field, find gaps in literature, and uncover connections between related studies.

Legal Document Analysis

Law firms and legal professionals can apply topic modeling to analyze large volumes of legal documents, contracts, and case law. This helps find relevant precedents, classify legal documents by topic, and automate the process of document review.

Overview of Unsupervised Techniques

Topic modeling is primarily based on unsupervised learning techniques, where the goal is to uncover hidden patterns in the data without using labeled examples. Unsupervised learning allows the model to discover the inherent structure in the data and make inferences based on statistical patterns rather than predefined labels.

One of the most widely used unsupervised learning techniques for topic modeling is Latent Dirichlet Allocation (LDA). LDA is a probabilistic model that assumes each document is a mixture of topics, with each topic being a distribution over words. The goal of LDA is to infer the topic distribution for each document and the word distribution for each topic, based on the observed data. LDA is particularly popular due to its simplicity and effectiveness in generating human-interpretable topics.

Another unsupervised learning technique is Non-Negative Matrix Factorization (NMF), which is used for dimensionality reduction in text. NMF decomposes the term-document matrix into two lower-dimensional matrices, one being the documents and the other being the terms. NMF has the advantage of producing non-negative factors, which can be easier to interpret when analyzing text data.

Additionally, more recent techniques, such as Latent Semantic Analysis (LSA) and various deep learning approaches, have been developed to improve the quality and interpretability of topic modeling. These techniques offer different methods of capturing latent semantic structures in text and are continually evolving with advances in NLP.

Review Questions

1. What is topic modeling, and how does it work?
2. How is topic modeling different from text classification?
3. Why is topic modeling useful for analyzing large text collections?
4. Name two real-world applications of topic modeling.
5. What does Latent Dirichlet Allocation (LDA) do?
6. What are some other techniques used for topic modeling besides LDA?

6-2 Latent Dirichlet Allocation (LDA)

Learning Outcomes

6-2-1 Explain what LDA is and how it finds topics in text.

6-2-2 Describe how documents are mixtures of topics and topics are mixtures of words.

6-2-3 Understand how LDA uses probability to assign topics to words.

6-2-4 Identify the key elements of LDA (documents, topics, words, Dirichlet).

6-2-5 Recognize the importance of choosing the right number of topics.

6-2-6 Know how to check if LDA topics make sense.

Latent Dirichlet Allocation (LDA) is a popular technique used to find hidden themes or "topics" in a collection of documents. The basic idea behind LDA is that each document is made up of a mixture of topics, and each topic is made up of a set of words. By analyzing many documents, LDA figures out which topics are present in each document and which words belong to each topic.

Probabilistic Topic Modeling

LDA works based on probabilistic topic modeling. This means that LDA treats the relationship between words, topics, and documents as a set of probabilities (which are based on relative frequencies). In simple terms, it guesses which topic a word in a document belongs to, based on patterns in the text. For example, if a document has words like "president" and "vote," LDA might guess it is about politics. The process of LDA is all about discovering these topics without knowing what they are ahead of time. It works by looking at which words tend to appear together and using that information to find topics that best explain the content of the documents.

How LDA Works

LDA Main Steps

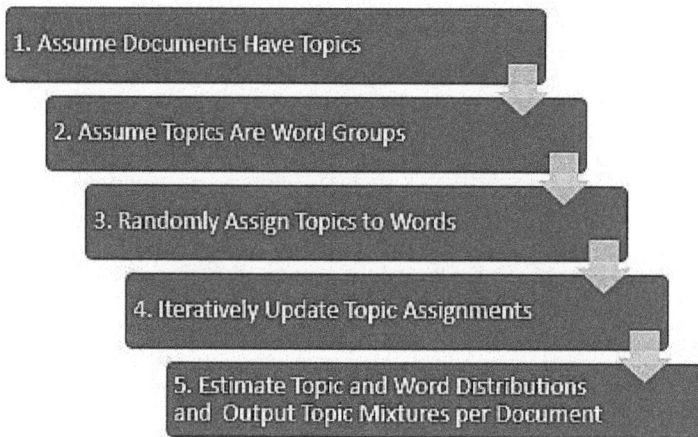

1. Assume Documents Have Topics

2. Assume Topics Are Word Groups

3. Randomly Assign Topics to Words

4. Iteratively Update Topic Assignments

5. Estimate Topic and Word Distributions and Output Topic Mixtures per Document

LDA follows a three-step process to figure out the topics in a set of documents. First, LDA randomly guesses what mix of topics could be in each document. For example, an article might be about sports and entertainment, so LDA might guess that 70% of the article is about sports and 30% is about entertainment. Once LDA has a mix of topics for the document, it looks at each word in the document and decides which topic it belongs to. For instance, if the word is "game," it might be assigned to a "sports" topic, but if the word is "movie," it might fit better with an "entertainment" topic.

After assigning topics to words, LDA then selects words based on the topic. Each topic has words that are more likely to appear in it. For example, a "sports" topic might include words like "team," "game," and "score," while an "entertainment" topic might include words like "actor," "movie," and "director." The goal of LDA is to uncover the hidden topics in a set of documents. It does this by repeating the process of guessing and refining until it has the best possible guess of what the topics are, and which words belong to each topic. This makes it easier to understand large sets of text without needing to read each document individually.

Why LDA is Useful

LDA is valuable because it helps us discover hidden themes in large collections of text. For example, if you have thousands of news articles, LDA can automatically find topics like "sports," "politics," or "entertainment" and tell you which topics are present in each article. This makes organizing and analyzing vast amounts of text much easier.

Key Components of LDA

The key parts of LDA are documents, topics, and words. A document is a mixture of different topics. For example, an article about politics might include topics like "elections," "government," and "laws," with some topics being more prominent than others. Topics are groups of words that often appear together. For instance, in a topic about politics, words like "election," "president," and "vote" might appear together. LDA discovers topics by noticing which words show up often in similar contexts. Words are the building blocks of topics. LDA assigns each word to a topic based on how likely it is to belong to that topic. For example, the word "president" is likely to be associated with the "politics" topic.

LDA uses a mathematical model called the Dirichlet distribution to make sure everything stays balanced. It helps decide how much of each topic should appear in a document and how words should fit into topics. This keeps everything organized, making sure the topics and words add up to 100% in each document and topic.

How LDA Assigns Topics

LDA assigns topics to documents based on probabilities. It looks at the words in a document, guesses which topics those words belong to, and refines its guesses over time. This process helps the LDA figure out the topics for each document. The way LDA works is like constantly guessing and adjusting. It keeps making better guesses about which topics fit which words and documents until it gets to a point where the guesses are very accurate.

Choosing the Right Number of Topics (K)

One challenge in using LDA is deciding how many topics it should look for, known as K. If K is too small, LDA might miss key details. If it is too large, the topics might be hard to understand. There are methods to help choose the right number of topics, such as looking at how well the model works with different numbers of topics. If you know a lot about the subject of the documents, you might have a good idea of how many topics there should be.

Evaluating LDA Models

To make sure LDA is working well, we need to evaluate the quality of the topics it finds. One way is to check how well LDA can predict the words in the documents. Another way is to see if the words in a topic make sense together. For example, a topic about politics should have words like "election," "vote," and "president" together. The topics should also be easy for people to understand and interpret.

LDA is a powerful tool for discovering hidden topics in substantial amounts of text. It works by figuring out the mix of topics in each document and selecting words based on those topics. By using probabilities and balancing techniques, LDA can uncover the underlying themes in an enormous collection of documents, making it easier to understand and organize big sets of text.

Example

Imagine a large company collects thousands of customer reviews about its products on an online store. The reviews are written in free text, and the company wants to understand the main themes customers are talking about—like product quality, delivery, or customer service—but there are too many reviews to read one by one. They use Latent Dirichlet Allocation (LDA) to automatically discover these hidden topics. LDA scans the reviews and notices that certain words often appear together. For example, reviews that mention "fast," "late," and "shipping" are grouped into a topic related to delivery. Another group of reviews with words like "broken," "quality," and "durable" might form a topic about product quality, while a third group with "refund," "support," and "helpful" is labeled as customer service. Each review may include a mix of these topics—one review might be 60delivery and 40 percent about product quality. LDA figures this out by assigning probabilities to words and topics based on how often they appear together across many reviews. The company can then use this information to identify common issues, improve products, and respond to customer needs more efficiently—without having to manually read every single review.

Review Questions

1. What is LDA used for?
2. How does LDA decide which topic a word belongs to?
3. What are the key parts of the LDA model?
4. Why is the number of topics (K) important in LDA?
5. How can we tell if the topics found by LDA are good?

6-3 Non-Negative Matrix Factorization

Non-Negative Matrix Factorization (NMF) is a powerful tool used to help us understand copious amounts of text. It helps find hidden themes or topics in a collection of documents, like books, articles, or even social media posts. When there is too much text to go through by hand, NMF can automatically figure out what the text is mostly about by grouping similar words together into topics. This makes it easier to analyze and organize large collections of text.

What is NMF?

Non-Negative Matrix Factorization, or NMF, is a method that breaks down large sets of data into smaller, easier-to-understand parts. Think of it like taking a giant puzzle and sorting the pieces into smaller sections. In the case of text, NMF looks at a bunch of documents and finds patterns in which words show up together. For example, words like "dog," "bone," and "tail" might be grouped together because they are often mentioned in documents about pets. NMF looks for these patterns and groups words that often appear together, which helps to find topics.

How Does NMF Work for Topic Modeling?

How NMF Works

1. Start with Term-Document Matrix

2. Decompose into Two Matrices and Constrain All Values to Be Positive

4. Interpret One Matrix as Topics

5. Interpret Other Matrix as Document-Topic Weights

6. Use for Topic Extraction

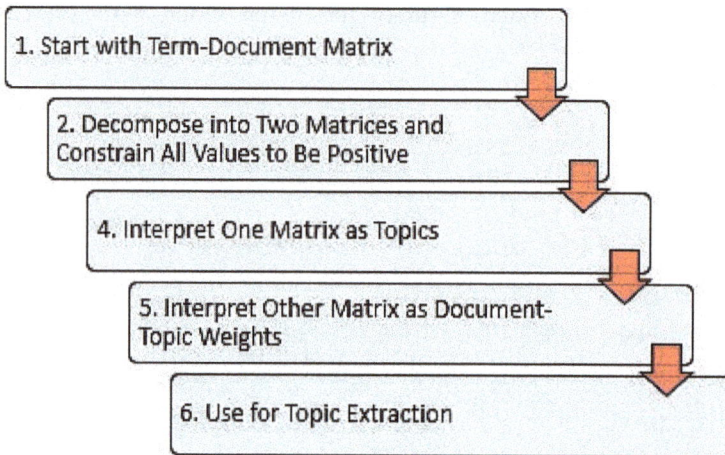

When you have an enormous collection of documents, NMF breaks the text into groups of related words, known as topics. For example, in a set of articles about different sports, NMF might find that words like "soccer," "goal," and "ball" often show up together, while words like "basketball," "hoop," and "court" belong to another topic. NMF groups these words into topics, so you end up with categories like "soccer" and "basketball."

Once the topics are found, NMF can also tell us which documents are most closely related to each topic. So, if a document is mostly about soccer, it will be labeled as related to the "soccer" topic. This makes it easier to see what each document is about without reading every single word.

Why is NMF Useful?

NMF is especially useful because it helps us quickly discover the main themes in a large collection of documents. Imagine you have thousands of news articles, and you want to know the main topics without reading each one. NMF can go through all the articles and figure out which ones are about sports, politics, health, or any other topic. It can automatically group the articles into these categories by looking at which words show up together.

This is helpful because it saves time and makes it easier to organize large sets of text. Whether it is used to improve search engines, recommend articles to people based on their interests, or sort through research papers, NMF can quickly find and organize the main topics in a huge amount of text.

Example

Imagine you have five short documents: one about a soccer game, one about basketball, one about a new diet, one about medical research, and one about a tennis match. NMF starts by creating a table that shows how often each word appears in each document—this is called a document-term matrix. All the values in this table are non-negative, meaning they are zero or higher (since you can't have a negative word count). Then, NMF breaks this big table into two smaller ones: one that shows how strongly each word belongs to each topic, and another that shows how strongly each document is related to each topic.

For example, the algorithm might find that the words "goal," "team," and "match" often appear together and label this group as Topic 1 (soccer). Another group with "hoop," "court," and "basketball" becomes Topic 2 (basketball). Similarly, it finds topics related to health, medicine, and tennis. Then, the algorithm looks at each document and sees which topics it matches best. If a document contains many words from Topic 1, it will have a high score for that topic and be considered mostly about soccer.

This process helps us automatically find themes in the documents and assign each one to one or more topics, depending on the words it uses. NMF is useful because it reduces a large amount of text into a few main ideas, making it much easier to organize and analyze.

Review Questions

1. What is NMF used for in topic modeling?
2. How does NMF group words together into topics?
3. How does NMF assign topics to documents?
4. Why is NMF useful for organizing large collections of text?

6-4 Latent Semantic Analysis

Learning Outcomes

6-4-1 Explain LSA and its use in finding topics in text.
6-4-2 Understand LSA's use of SVD for word relationships.
6-4-3 Recognize how LSA reduces data complexity.
6-4-4 Identify strengths and limitations of LSA.

Latent Semantic Analysis (LSA) is a technique used to help computers understand text. It is commonly employed to find hidden meanings or topics in large collections of documents, such as articles or books. By analyzing patterns in how words are used together, LSA uncovers topics or themes that are not directly stated but are implied in the text. This technique is helpful because it reduces the complexity of text data while keeping the most essential information intact, making it easier to analyze and draw insights from.

How LSA Works

How LSA Works

1. Create Term-Document Matrix

2. Apply Singular Value Decomposition (SVD)

3. Reduce to Fewer Dimensions

4. Group Words and Documents by Meaning

5. Identify Latent Semantic Topics and Use Topics for Analysis or Retrieval

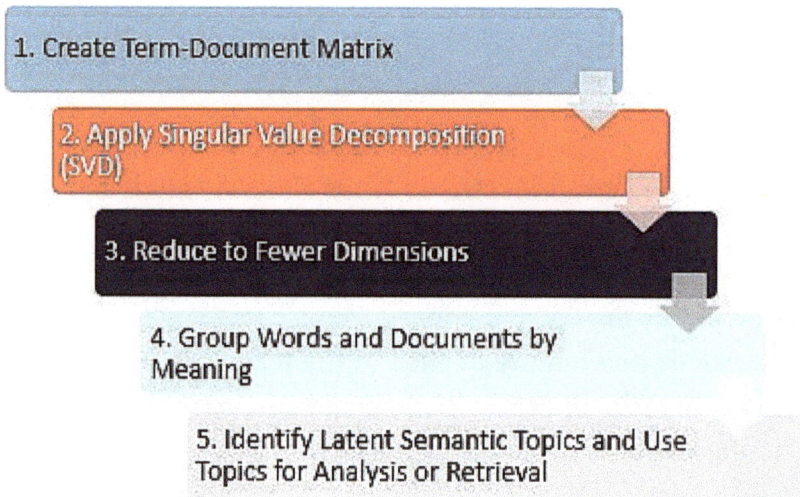

LSA works by examining the relationships between words across a collection of documents. It uses on the idea that words used in similar contexts often share similar meanings. For instance, if words like "dog," "bone," and "tail" often appear together, LSA would recognize that these words are related to the topic of pets or animals. To achieve this, LSA employs a mathematical technique called Singular Value Decomposition (SVD), which breaks down the text data into smaller components. This allows the system to focus on the most important relationships between words. By using SVD, LSA reduces the complexity of the data, making it easier to extract useful topics or themes.

Dimensionality Reduction and Topic Extraction

One of LSA's main strengths is its ability to simplify large amounts of data, which allows it to find topics more easily. In a large collection of documents, many words might not appear in every document. For example, in a book about science, the word "biology" might appear only in some chapters. LSA helps to reduce this "noise" by focusing only on the most important patterns of word usage. When LSA reduces the complexity of the data, it groups words into topics that stand for these patterns. While these topics may not be at once obvious, they are inferred based on how often certain words appear together. For instance, if many documents mention words like "vote," "election," and "campaign," LSA might group these words into a topic about politics.

Strengths and Limitations of LSA

Latent Semantic Analysis (LSA) brings several useful advantages to the table. One of its main strengths lies in how efficiently it can handle large volumes of text. By simplifying the underlying structure of the data, LSA can work through vast collections of documents at a relatively fast pace. It's also good at filtering out less important details, allowing more focus on the core ideas or themes. Another valuable aspect is its ability to detect subtle connections between words, which can reveal deeper insights into what the text is really about.

That said, LSA isn't perfect. While it can identify patterns that point to underlying topics, those topics aren't always easy to interpret. Because LSA relies more on mathematical techniques than on the rules of language, the results can be abstract or unclear without additional explanation. It can also become less practical with extremely large datasets, since the process of breaking down and summarizing the data can require significant computing power. On top of that, LSA tends to struggle with words that have more than one meaning, which may lead to ambiguity in some cases.

> **Example**
>
> Imagine you have five documents: one about climate change, one about elections, one about pollution, one about voting rights, and one about renewable energy. LSA looks at all the words in these documents and builds a table showing how often each word appears in each document—this is the document-term matrix. Next, LSA uses a mathematical method called Singular Value Decomposition (SVD) to break that matrix into smaller pieces. This process finds hidden patterns in how words are used across different documents, even if they don't always appear together. For example, LSA might notice that "carbon," "emissions," and "pollution" tend to appear in similar documents and are related to environmental topics. It may also find that "vote," "ballot," and "election" often occur together, pointing to a political topic.
>
> After applying SVD, LSA reduces the number of dimensions—or word patterns—it needs to consider, which makes the data simpler and easier to analyze. This helps group related words into topics and shows how closely each document is connected to those topics. For instance, the document about renewable energy may partly relate to the environmental topic and partly to a political topic if it also discusses government policy. While LSA is powerful in finding hidden relationships, the topics it finds aren't always clear-cut. For example, it might group "power" with both "electricity" and "voting," which could be confusing. Still, LSA is very useful when you want to explore the overall themes in large text collections without reading each document.

Review Questions

1. What is LSA used for?
2. How does LSA work with SVD?
3. How does LSA reduce text complexity?
4. What are LSA's strengths and weaknesses?

6-5 Applications of Topic Modeling

Learning Outcomes

6-5-1 Identify real-world uses of topic modeling.
6-5-2 Understand how topic modeling helps organize and analyze large text data.

Topic modeling is a powerful technique used in Natural Language Processing (NLP) to discover hidden thematic structures in large collections of text data. This process has become increasingly important across various industries for extracting meaningful insights from vast amounts of unstructured data.

Real World Uses of Topic Modelling

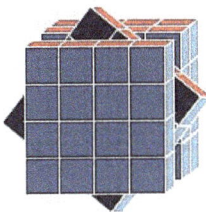

01 Customer Feedback Analysis

02 Social Media Monitoring

03 Content Recommendation

04 Academic Research

05 Legal Document Review

News Categorization

One of the key applications of topic modeling in the news industry is news categorization. News outlets generate a constant flow of articles covering diverse topics. For readers and news organizations alike, organizing and categorizing this information effectively is critical. Topic modeling techniques, such as Latent Dirichlet Allocation (LDA) and Latent Semantic Analysis (LSA), can be used to automatically extract themes from news articles.

By applying topic modeling to large collections of news reports, organizations can classify articles into categories such as politics, sports, business, health, and entertainment. This can help readers quickly find articles relevant to their interests without manually sorting them through numerous sources. Moreover, topic modeling allows for the identification of emerging trends in news reporting. By tracking how topics evolve over time, news organizations can uncover shifts in public interest, new developments in ongoing stories, and potential areas of coverage that may have been overlooked. This dynamic process offers a way to capture the ever-changing nature of news reporting, offering valuable insights for both content producers and consumers.

Academic and Scientific Research

Topic modeling has proven particularly useful in the realm of academic and scientific research. Researchers often deal with a vast amount of published literature across various disciplines. Manually reviewing each research paper for relevant themes or connections can be a daunting task, but topic modeling offers a way to automate this process.

One of the main applications of topic modeling in research is analyzing large-scale research papers. By applying topic modeling to academic articles, researchers can automatically discover underlying topics within vast bodies of literature. This can help researchers find which topics are receiving the most attention in each field, track the evolution of ideas over time, and pinpoint gaps in the research that may require further exploration.

Additionally, automatic document clustering can be performed to help with literature reviews. Topic modeling algorithms can group research papers with similar themes, making it easier for researchers to access relevant studies quickly. This is particularly useful when reviewing large sets of papers for specific subfields, where manually sorting through individual documents would be time-consuming and inefficient. By using topic modeling, researchers can gain deeper insights into trends within their area of study and find key themes that are central to ongoing research.

Social Media Analysis

Social media platforms like Twitter and Reddit generate massive amounts of textual data daily. Social media analysis using topic modeling can offer valuable insights into public sentiment and trending topics, making it a useful tool for businesses, governments, and researchers alike.

Topic modeling is often employed for discovering trending topics on platforms like Twitter. By analyzing the content of tweets over a period, topic modeling algorithms can find which topics are gaining traction among users. This can be especially useful for marketers and businesses looking to understand public opinion or measure the success of a specific campaign. For instance, during a political event, topic modeling can find key issues that are being discussed, such as healthcare, economy, or foreign policy, and how the public feels about these issues.

Moreover, topic modeling can also be used to show public sentiment on various issues. By analyzing the tone and themes of social media posts, businesses and governments can assess the public's reaction to a product launch, a political debate, or a societal event. For example, analyzing Twitter posts following a major news event can reveal whether the public is supportive, critical, or neutral toward the event. This real-time feedback is invaluable for decision-makers who need to quickly understand the public's stance on an issue and adjust their strategies accordingly.

Legal and Business Intelligence

In the fields of legal and business intelligence, topic modeling has been a game-changer for tasks that require processing large volumes of text data, such as contract analysis, document classification, and fraud detection.

One significant application is in contract analysis. Legal teams often deal with large collections of contracts and legal documents that need to be reviewed for specific clauses, terms, or conditions. Topic modeling can automatically find relevant clauses related to specific legal terms, helping legal professionals efficiently navigate and classify the documents. This also aids in spotting potential risks or inconsistencies that may require further attention, such as problematic language or clauses that need renegotiation.

In the realm of document classification, businesses can use topic modeling to sort and categorize their internal documents, such as reports, memos, and communications, into themes or topics. This makes it easier to retrieve documents related to specific business functions, such as marketing, finance, or operations, streamlining internal processes and improving organizational efficiency.

Topic modeling is also used to detect fraud and compliance risks in financial reports. Financial institutions often have vast amounts of regulatory documents, reports, and statements that need to be watched for compliance. By applying topic modeling to these documents, it is possible to uncover patterns that show fraudulent activity or non-compliance with regulations. For instance, discrepancies in financial statements, unusual patterns in transaction data, or deviations from industry standards can be flagged for further investigation.

Review Questions

1. How can topic modeling be used in news categorization?
2. What are the key applications of topic modeling in academic research?
3. How does topic modeling help in analyzing social media content?
4. How is topic modeling applied in legal and business intelligence tasks?

Chapter 7

Text Classification

7-1 Supervised Learning and NLP

Learning Outcomes

7-1-1 Define text classification and supervised learning.
7-1-2 List common uses like spam detection and sentiment analysis.
7-1-3 Know why labeled data is important.

Supervised learning is a key technique in Natural Language Processing (NLP) that involves training machine learning models to classify text based on labeled data. Text classification, a critical application of supervised learning, has widespread use in a variety of fields, from spam detection in emails to sentiment analysis of customer feedback.

Define Text Classification

Text classification is the process of categorizing text into predefined labels or classes. This task involves training a machine learning model to classify a given piece of text into one of several categories based on its content. Examples of text classification include classifying emails as "spam" or "not spam," deciding whether a tweet expresses "positive" or "negative" sentiment, and categorizing news articles into topics such as "politics," "sports," or "business." The goal of text classification is to assign labels to text data that make it easier to process, analyze, and retrieve relevant information.

For instance, in a spam detection system, an email is categorized as either "spam" or "not spam" based on its content, specific words or phrases that commonly appear in spam messages. Similarly, sentiment analysis involves classifying text as expressing positive, negative, or neutral sentiment, which is particularly useful for understanding customer feedback.

Importance of Text Classification

Text classification has a wide range of practical applications across various industries. These applications help automate the organization and interpretation of text, making it easier for businesses and organizations to manage large volumes of data. Below are three key examples that highlight the importance of text classification.

Email Filtering (Spam Detection)

One of the most common and practical applications of text classification is in email filtering, specifically for spam detection. The purpose of spam detection is to classify incoming emails as either "spam" or "not spam." With the increasing volume of email traffic, it is essential to ensure that users are not overwhelmed by irrelevant or potentially harmful messages. By employing text classification models that are trained on labeled data, email providers can automatically find and filter out spam messages. This not only enhances the user experience by reducing clutter but also helps protect users from harmful content such as phishing attacks or malware.

Sentiment Analysis

Another critical application of text classification is sentiment analysis, which is especially useful in customer service and social media monitoring. Companies use sentiment analysis to assess customer feelings from various text sources such as reviews, feedback, or social media posts. By categorizing text as expressing positive, negative, or neutral sentiment, businesses can gain valuable insights into how customers perceive their products or services. For example, analyzing customer reviews allows companies to find recurring complaints, areas needing improvement, or features that customers love. This information can then be used to improve products, enhance customer satisfaction, or adjust marketing strategies.

Topic Classification

Topic classification is essential for organizing content, particularly news articles, blogs, and other forms of written material. In this application, text classification models categorize content into predefined topics such as "sports," "politics," "technology," or "health." This method helps readers easily find relevant content and ensures that automated systems can efficiently process substantial amounts of text. For instance, news websites and aggregators use topic classification models to automatically sort articles, enabling users to access information on specific topics that match their interests. This improves content accessibility and enhances the overall user experience on news platforms.

Review Questions

1. What is text classification?
2. Give two uses of text classification.
3. Why do we need labeled data?

7-2 Supervised Learning Basics

Supervised learning is a type of machine learning where the model is trained on a labeled dataset, meaning that the data used for training includes both the input features (text) and the corresponding target labels (categories). The goal is to learn a mapping from inputs to outputs so that the model can predict the correct label for unseen text. Supervised learning involves three key components: labeled datasets, feature extraction techniques, and evaluation metrics.

Labeled Datasets

In supervised learning, labeled datasets are essential for training models. These datasets consist of text documents paired with corresponding labels, which are used to teach the model the relationship between input text and its category. For example, in a spam detection system, the dataset would consist of a collection of emails with labels saying whether each email is spam or not. The model learns patterns in the text that correlate with the assigned labels, which it can then apply to new, unseen data.

Labeled Data

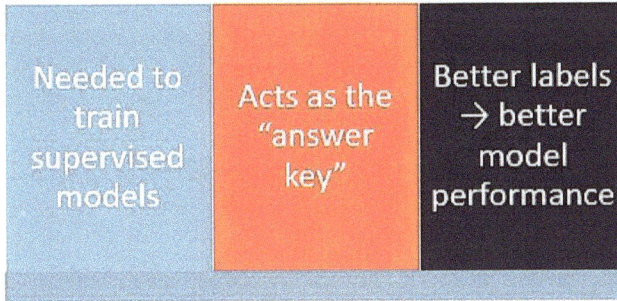

| Needed to train supervised models | Acts as the "answer key" | Better labels → better model performance |

The process of labeling data is often time-consuming and requires domain knowledge, but it is crucial for the model's ability to generalize and perform well on real-world tasks. Labeled datasets serve as the foundation for training and evaluating text classification models, and their quality directly affects model performance.

Feature Extraction Techniques

Feature extraction is the process of transforming raw text into numerical representations that machine learning models can process. There are several popular techniques for extracting features from text.

Feature Extraction Methods

- Bag of Words (BoW) *Word frequency*
- TF-IDF *Weights important terms*
- Word Embeddings *Semantic meaning*

Bag of Words (BoW)

This is one of the simplest and most widely used methods for text feature extraction. In the BoW model, each document is represented as a vector of word frequencies, where each element in the vector corresponds to the count of a specific word in the document. While BoW is simple and effective, it does not capture word order or context, which can be a limitation for certain applications.

TF-IDF (Term Frequency-Inverse Document Frequency)

TF-IDF improves BoW by weighing words based on their importance within a document compared to the entire corpus. It reduces the weight of familiar words (like "the," "and," etc.) that appear often across documents and emphasizes words that are unique to specific documents. This helps the model focus on more informative features.

Word Embeddings

Word embeddings, such as Word2Vec, GloVe, and FastText, represent words as dense vectors in a continuous vector space. Unlike BoW and TF-IDF, word embeddings capture semantic relationships between words. Words with similar meanings are mapped to nearby points in the vector space, making this approach particularly effective for tasks where word context matters, such as sentiment analysis or named entity recognition.

Evaluation Metrics

Once a text classification model has been trained, it is essential to evaluate its performance using various evaluation metrics. Common metrics used for supervised learning in NLP include:

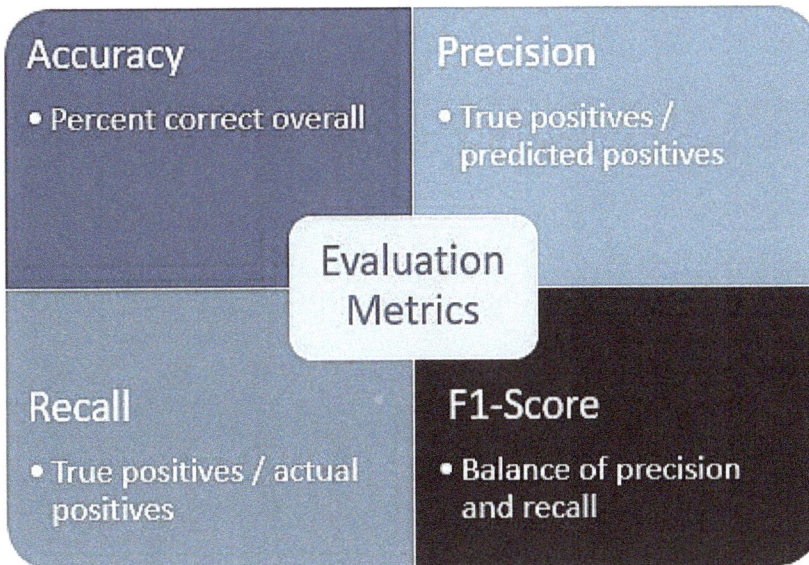

Accuracy
- Percent correct overall

Precision
- True positives / predicted positives

Evaluation Metrics

Recall
- True positives / actual positives

F1-Score
- Balance of precision and recall

Accuracy

Accuracy measures the overall percentage of correctly classified instances. While it is simple to calculate, it may not be sufficient for imbalanced datasets where some classes dominate over others.

Precision

Precision calculates the proportion of true positive results among all instances classified as positive. It is particularly useful in scenarios where false positives (incorrectly labeling a negative instance as positive) are costly or undesirable.

Recall

Recall measures the proportion of true positive results among all actual positive instances. It is important when the cost of missing a positive instance (false negative) is high, such as in medical diagnosis or fraud detection.

F1-Score

The F1-score is the harmonic mean of precision and recall, providing a balanced measure of a model's performance when both false positives and false negatives are of concern. It is often used when dealing with imbalanced classes or when both precision and recall are important.

Review Questions

1. What is the purpose of a labeled dataset in supervised learning?
2. Name two methods for extracting features from text.
3. When is F1-score more useful than accuracy?

7-3 Naïve Bayes for Text Classification

Naïve Bayes is a simple but powerful machine learning algorithm that's commonly used for text classification. It uses a concept called Bayes' theorem, which helps predict the likelihood of a document belonging to a certain category based on the words in it. Even though it is a simple method, Naïve Bayes works well for many tasks like spam filtering, sentiment analysis, and organizing documents.

Introduction to Naïve Bayes

Naïve Bayes is based on Bayes' theorem, which is a way to calculate the probability of an event happening based on related events. In text classification, Bayes' theorem helps us calculate the chance of a document belonging to a certain category by looking at the words in it. The formula used in Naïve Bayes looks at the relationship between the category and the features (words).

The key assumption of Naïve Bayes is that all the words in a document are independent of each other, which makes calculations easier. While words in a text are usually connected in real language, this assumption works well in many cases and helps keep things simple.

Types of Naïve Bayes Models

There are different types of Naïve Bayes models, each designed for different kinds of text data. The three main types are:

The Multinomial Naïve Bayes model is the commonly used version of Naïve Bayes for text classification. It is good when the frequency of words matters. For example, if certain words like "free" or "offer" appear a lot in an email, it might be a sign that the email is spam. This model looks at how often these words appear to decide if an email is spam or not.

The Bernoulli Naïve Bayes model works differently. Instead of looking at how often a word appears, it looks at whether a word is present in the document at all. This model is useful for tasks like sentiment analysis, where we care more about the presence of certain words (like "happy" or "good") to decide if something is positive or negative.

The Gaussian Naïve Bayes model is used when the features are continuous, meaning they are not just words or categories but numbers. For example, it can be used when dealing with data that has numbers, like ratings or scores. This version is not as commonly used for text classification, but it can be helpful in certain situations where data is continuous.

Advantages and Limitations

Naïve Bayes

Pros	Cons
• Fast and simple • Works well with small data • Ignores irrelevant features	• Assumes word independence • Poor with complex grammar/context

Naïve Bayes is often a practical option for sorting text into categories because of its speed and simplicity. It performs reliably even when only a small amount of data is available, unlike some more advanced techniques that require large datasets. One of its key advantages is that it can handle noisy data fairly well, often ignoring unimportant words that don't contribute much to the overall meaning.

That said, it's not without flaws. A major drawback is its underlying assumption that every word in a document appears independently of the others—something that rarely holds true in real-world language. In most cases, words influence one another based on grammar and context. As a result, Naïve Bayes can fall short when tackling tasks that involve understanding sentence structure or subtle meaning. More sophisticated approaches, such as neural networks, are usually better suited for those challenges.

All in all, while Naïve Bayes is a solid starting point for many text analysis problems, it isn't ideal for handling complex linguistic relationships. It excels in straightforward scenarios but has trouble grasping deeper layers of meaning in language

---

Example

A small online bookstore was struggling with customer feedback. They received hundreds of product reviews every week, and the team wanted a quick way to understand which reviews were positive and which were negative. Manually reading all the reviews took too much time, so they decided to use a machine learning tool to help sort the reviews automatically. They chose the Naïve Bayes algorithm because it was simple, fast, and worked well with text.

The team collected around 2,000 past customer reviews, each labeled as either positive or negative. Many positive reviews used words like "great," "easy to read," and "loved it," while negative reviews often included words like "boring," "disappointed," or "poor quality." After cleaning the text by removing punctuation and turning everything lowercase, they converted the words into a numerical format so the model could process them.

They trained a Multinomial Naïve Bayes classifier on this data. This type of model looks at how often each word appears in the reviews and uses that information to make predictions. After training, they tested the model on 500 new, unlabeled reviews to see how well it worked. The results were promising: the model correctly labeled 91It was especially good at spotting clearly positive or negative language.

Thanks to the Naïve Bayes model, the bookstore team could now sort through customer reviews automatically. Positive reviews were flagged to highlight on the product pages, while negative ones were sent to cus-

---

tomer service for follow-up. This saved time, helped improve customer satisfaction, and gave the business a simple but effective tool for understanding customer opinions.

Review Questions

1. What does Naïve Bayes assume about the words in a document?
2. Which version of Naïve Bayes is most common for text classification?
3. Name one advantage and one limitation of using Naïve Bayes for NLP.

7-4 SVM for Text Classification

Learning Outcomes

7-4-1 Explain how Support Vector Machines (SVM) classify text using hyperplanes.
7-4-2 Describe the role of support vectors and the kernel trick in SVM.
7-4-3 Identify common kernel types and explain when to use them.
7-4-4 Discuss why SVM is effective for high-dimensional text data.

Support Vector Machines (SVM) are a popular tool in machine learning, especially when it comes to sorting things into different categories, such as labeling emails as spam or not spam, figuring out the mood of a sentence (like whether a review is positive or negative), or classifying articles into topics like sports or politics. Imagine you have a bunch of data points, and you want to draw a line or boundary that separates these points into two groups. SVM helps you do this in a way that ensures the boundary you draw has the biggest gap possible between the two groups, so that the system can be sure which group each new point belongs to.

The Basic Idea of SVM

At its core, SVM works by trying to find the best way to separate different categories of data. This separation is done by drawing something called a "hyperplane" – which you can think of as a fancy way of saying a boundary or dividing line. The goal is to find this line or boundary in such a way that there is the biggest possible gap between the points of each category. In other words, SVM tries to draw the line where the data points from one group are as far away from the line as possible, while also making sure the other group is also as far away as possible.

The Challenge with Text Data

When dealing with text, things can get a bit trickier. Text data, like emails or news articles, can be complex and high-dimensional. This means that instead of just dealing with a few simple categories, you might be working with thousands of different words, phrases, or features. This makes it difficult for some algorithms to handle. SVM, however, is good at dealing with this complexity. Even though the text data may seem messy or overwhelming, SVM is designed to efficiently find that dividing line, or hyperplane, which will help classify the text correctly.

Support Vectors

Now, imagine that there are some points in the dataset that are closest to the boundary or line that SVM draws. These points are called "support vectors." Think of them as the most important points in deciding where to draw the boundary. The job of SVM is to find these key support vectors and make sure they are on opposite sides of the boundary, so it can separate the data correctly.

How SVM Handles Non-Straightforward Data

In the real world, data is not always neatly separated by a straight line. For example, if you want to classify movie reviews into positive and negative categories, it might not be easy to draw a straight line between the two. Some reviews might be positive but have some negative words, and vice versa. SVM solves this problem using something called the "kernel trick." The kernel trick helps SVM by transforming the data into a higher-dimensional space where the data points can be separated by a straight line. So, even if the data looks like it is too complex or "curvy" to be separated with a straight line, the kernel trick makes it easier to classify the data.

Different Types of Kernels

There are different ways to use the kernel trick, depending on how complex the data is. For simple problems, SVM can use what is called a "linear kernel." This is like drawing a straight line to separate the data. For example, if you are classifying emails as spam or not spam based on words like "sale" or "buy," a linear kernel might be enough.

However, for more complex problems, like deciding whether a tweet is happy or sad, a more advanced kernel may be needed. One choice is the polynomial kernel, which helps the algorithm find more complex patterns between words in the text. Another powerful option is the radial basis function (RBF) kernel, which maps the data to an infinite-dimensional space, allowing SVM to find even more complex boundaries and making it particularly effective for text data.

Why SVM is Great for Text Classification

Advantages of SVM

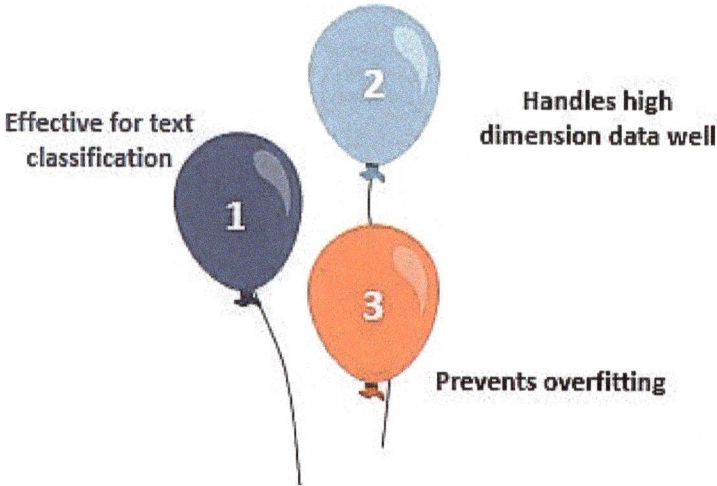

Effective for text classification

2

Handles high dimension data well

1

3

Prevents overfitting

SVM is great for text classification because it works well with text data's large size and complexity. For example, if you are classifying thousands of product reviews, SVM can handle the high number of words used across different reviews, separating positive and negative reviews effectively. Another reason SVM works well for text is its ability to avoid "overfitting." This is a problem where a machine learning model gets too caught up in the details of the training data and does not perform well on new data. SVM avoids this by focusing on the key support vectors and drawing the most reliable boundaries.

Example

A popular online clothing store was receiving hundreds of customer reviews every day, and they wanted to automate the process of categorizing them into positive and negative reviews. Sorting through them manually was too time-consuming, so they decided to use a machine learning model, Support Vector Machines (SVM), to help.

SVM works by drawing a line, or boundary, that separates the reviews into two groups: positive and negative. The goal was to find the best line that would ensure that the reviews in each category were as far apart as possible. In other words, the SVM algorithm aimed to draw the line where the positive reviews were on one side and the negative reviews were on the other, with as much space between them as possible.

However, classifying reviews based on their text isn't always straightforward. Some positive reviews might mention a few negative words, and some negative reviews could have positive language. To tackle this, the team used SVM's kernel trick. This technique helped the model transform the data into a higher-dimensional space, where it was easier to find a line that could separate the reviews, even if they were messy or complex.

After training the model on a sample of reviews, SVM was able to correctly classify new reviews. It used support vectors, which are the key reviews closest to the dividing line, to help decide where to draw the boundary. In this case, SVM handled the large number of words in each review and classified them effectively into positive or negative categories. This allowed the store to automatically highlight positive feedback and forward negative reviews to customer service.

By using SVM, the clothing store saved time and was able to automate the classification of customer reviews with great accuracy, making it easier to respond to customers and improve their shopping experience.

Review Questions

1. What does an SVM try to maximize when drawing a boundary between classes?
2. What are support vectors, and why are they important?
3. How does the kernel trick help SVM handle complex data?
4. Name two types of kernels used in SVM and describe when each might be useful.
5. Why is SVM a good choice for classifying text data?

7-5 Logistic Regression for Text Classification

Learning Outcomes

7-5-1 Explain how logistic regression classifies text.
7-5-2 Describe the sigmoid function and decision-making.
7-5-3 Identify how features are weighted.
7-5-4 Compare logistic regression with Naïve Bayes and SVM.

Logistic Regression is a popular and easy-to-understand machine learning method used for text classification. It is a powerful tool often used for tasks like finding spam emails, analyzing sentiment (like positive or negative reviews), and categorizing topics.

What is Logistic Regression?

Logistic regression is a type of machine learning algorithm that helps categorize data into one of two categories. For example, in a spam detection task, logistic regression can help decide whether an email is spam or not. It calculates the chance (or probability) that the email belongs to either category (spam or not spam). Based on this probability, it makes its final decision.

How Logistic Regression Works

At the core of logistic regression is something called the "sigmoid function." This function takes any number and turns it into a value between 0 and 1. In text classification, this value is the probability of a document belonging to a certain category. For example, if the function gives a value closer to one, it suggests that the document is likely to belong to the category "spam." If the value is closer to zero, the document is more likely to belong to the "not spam" category.

Making Decisions with Logistic Regression

The decision of whether a document belongs to one category, or another is made based on the probability that logistic regression predicts. If the probability is higher than 0.5, the document is classified into one category (e.g., spam), and if it is lower, it goes into the other category (e.g., not spam). This threshold can be adjusted to balance the importance of precision (correctly finding spam) and recall (catching as many spam emails as possible).

Understanding Feature Importance

One of the strengths of logistic regression is that it helps us understand which features (like words in a document) are most important for classification. It does this by giving each feature a weight during the learning process.

Features that strongly indicate a particular category get a higher weight. For example, the word "free" might have a high weight in a spam detection task because it often appears in spam emails. On the other hand, words like "unsubscribe" might have a low weight, as they are more common in non-spam emails.

How Regularization Helps

Regularization is a technique used in logistic regression to prevent overfitting, which happens when the model works too well on the training data but does not make correct predictions on new data. There are two types of regularization in logistic regression: L1 (Lasso) and L2 (Ridge).

L1 regularization removes unnecessary features by forcing their weights to become zero, which helps the model focus only on the most important features. L2 regularization, on the other hand, reduces the impact of features with very large weights, ensuring that the model doesn't over-rely on any one feature.

Comparing to Other Models

Advantage of Logistic Models

Flexible	Fast and Simple	Small Data
• More flexible than Naïve Bayes (no independence assumption)	• Simpler and faster than SVM	• Suitable for straightforward, smaller datasets

Logistic regression is often compared with other machine learning methods like Naïve Bayes and Support Vector Machines (SVM). Each of these methods has strengths that make them suitable for different tasks.

Naïve Bayes works well when the features are independent of each other, but this assumption doesn't always hold true in real-world text data. Logistic regression does not make this assumption, which makes it more flexible for tasks where the relationship between words and categories is more complex.

When compared to SVM, logistic regression is simpler and easier to understand. SVM can handle more complex data, especially when there are a lot of features or when the data isn't easily separable. However, logistic regression is faster and works well when the data is simple and straightforward.

Logistic regression is a great choice for text classification tasks when you need a simple, interpretable model that works well with smaller or straightforward datasets. It is a good choice for tasks like spam detection and sentiment analysis, where the relationships between the data points are simple. For more complex tasks, SVM or Naïve Bayes might be better, depending on the situation.

Example

A small digital marketing agency wanted to improve how they handled client feedback. Every month, clients left reviews about the agency's services, but it was hard to determine quickly whether the feedback was positive or negative. Instead of reading each review manually, they decided to use a machine learning method called Logistic Regression to automatically classify the reviews as either "positive" or "negative."

To train the model, they collected 1,500 past reviews, which were already labeled as positive or negative. They then used the logistic regression algorithm, which works by calculating the probability that a review belongs to one category or the other. In this case, the model would determine the likelihood that a review was positive or negative based on the words it contained. The algorithm uses something called a sigmoid function, which outputs a value between 0 and 1. If the output was closer to 1, the review was likely positive; closer to 0, the review was negative.

Once the model was trained, it could automatically classify new reviews. For example, a review that said, "I love how quick and professional the team was!" would likely be classified as positive, while "I am unhappy with the slow service" would be classified as negative. The agency set a threshold of 0.5: If the probability was greater than 0.5, the review was classified as positive; otherwise, it was negative.

One of the benefits of logistic regression was that the agency could also see which words played a big role in determining the review's sentiment. For instance, words like "quick" and "professional" were given high weights, making them important indicators of positive feedback. Words like "slow" and "unhappy" were weighted heavily for negative reviews.

The agency also applied regularization to prevent overfitting. By using L1 regularization, the model focused on the most relevant words, ignoring less important ones. This made sure the model didn't rely too much on any single word, keeping its predictions more reliable across different reviews.

By using logistic regression, the marketing agency was able to automatically sort and analyze customer feedback much faster than before. This helped them respond quickly to both positive reviews (by thanking clients) and negative ones (by addressing issues) while improving customer satisfaction and streamlining their workflow.

Review Questions

1. What is the role of the sigmoid function?
2. How does logistic regression classify text?
3. What do L1 and L2 regularization do?
4. How are important words identified?
5. When is logistic regression a good choice?

www.ingramcontent.com/pod-product-compliance
Lightning Source LLC
Chambersburg PA
CBHW051857210326
41597CB00033B/5930